W9-AYQ-283

As The Twig
Is Bent
by
Elinor C. Bemis

These essays appeared
originally in the *York County Coast Star*
from 1984 to 1986

I wish to thank the *Star*
for its assistance and cooperation
in the publication
of this book.

A WINDSWEPT BOOK
Windswept House Publishers
Mount Desert, Maine 04660

Printed in the United
States of America
for the Publisher by
Downeast Graphics & Printing, Inc.
Ellsworth, Maine

For LDB
welcome to New Hampshire
Christmas 1995

As The Twig Is Bent

Tis education forms the common mind;
Just as the twig is bent, the tree's inclined.
—Alexander Pope

THE COLE SISTERS

Dorothy Eliza   *Elizabeth Florence*   *Elinor Francis*

Introduction

I was raised in an atmosphere of proverbs, superstitions, homemade bread and the New Deal. The influence of the Puritans nourished the precepts of my upbringing as surely as an underground river feeds the roots reaching down in the earth. Outward expressions of love, as well as any manifestation of weakness, were stoically and from long habit and tradition, repressed.

A depth of security compensated. There was the farm, a world of its own, slumbering in the somnolent summer heat; locked in the dazzling crystal of a snowbound winter; murmuring in the awakening of early spring; drowsing in the heavy scent of dying autumn leaves, the full moon slanting through the rustling branches of the hovering elms.

I can only guess at my father's disappointment when I was born — another girl to make three. A farmer, lumberman, wood dealer and market gardener, he needed a son or two, to raise in the tradition of his ancestors, to share the burdens and chores; to carry on his name.

My mother was nearly 40 years old when I was born; by my fifth birthday, two things were evident — I would be my parent's last child and was destined to be a tomboy.

I write for the grandfather who never saw the sun slant through the avenue of maple trees he planted, one by one on grass-stained knees so many years ago; for my father and the son he never had, to ease the ache of a name gone dead; for the mother who held secret dreams unhearkened by callous ears through years of toil and dirt and care.

Most of all I write for all the little country girls with barked knees who grew up in a world of innocence and artless simplicity long perished from the earth.

ELINOR

This book is dedicated
to my friend
Barbara J. Morell,
whose inspiration and generosity
made possible the publication of
this book.

SPRING

Breaking the Bonds

It was very close to spring on the calendar. All around the farm, signs of the blossoming season forecast the end of winter as surely as the wild, restless winds, the changing quality of light and air.

A crocus bloomed against the warmth of the gray granite front step; pussy willows lined the swamp edge; the shrinking snow piles in the shadowed corners of the ell retreated a little each day.

On the dried, brown hillsides, the lambs frolicked, jumping, tossing their heads, prancing sidewise in delight. Their carefree antics expressed the very essence of the joy of spring — a jubilation shared by wild creatures and humans alike.

A change was in the air; winter's icy fingers still clung, holding us back, but the turbulence of March aroused strange impulses. An urge deep within impelled us, like the lambs, to kick up our heels.

My mother would spend too much on a new hat for Easter; my father would send an order for a packet of an exotic, unproven seed; Old Man Ellis would get drunk and fall in a ditch on the way home. Maurice would skip school to go fishing. The hired man would put on a string tie, grease his hair and go sparking.

The March wind blew in these confusions, these unspoken yearnings. In due time, it would blow them out, leaving us to get on with the mud, warmth and reckless blooming, the busyness of spring.

On the way to school, as surely as a snake sloughs off its old skin, I shed my plaid wool winter jacket, stuffing it in the hollow tree beside the brook, ignoring the chill that cut through my sweater.

The schoolroom was extra noisy; a piece of green wood hissed and bubbled in the stove; there was the sound of fidgety feet scraping the wooden floor; the hacking of lingering winter coughs; the rattle of inkwell covers.

At recess, I ran back into the classroom to get my mittens from my lunchbox. Miss Crosby sat at her desk, buffing her perfect pink nails with an ivory-handled white kid buffer. Spread out on her planning book were the several other tiny ivory-handled implements that made up a ladies "nail set."

Quickly and surreptitiously, she covered them over with an arithmetic book, assuming her most professional look in spite of the blush that colored her cheeks at being caught in the act. Pretending to be grading papers, she ignored my presence.

I knew she would be in real trouble if a member of the school committee had found her performing such an act of "personal toilette" in public, breaching the established rules of decorum. She, too, was kicking over the traces, I thought, and liked her all the better for it.

My jacket had a damp, musty odor as I pulled it out of the tree trunk, shrugged into it and plodded home, unbuckled overshoes flapping. My hands were cold and red from building dams in the streams of melting snow in the schoolyard.

Ice was already skimming the puddles as the sun dropped behind the pines to the west, but at the edge of the meadow the sturdy purple globes of skunk cabbage were a stronger omen.

A red-winged blackbird swayed on the bare brown stalk of a cattail; a pair of ducks flew in, landing on the still, black water of the pond.

It was all beginning again, just as it always had. There was a certainty about spring.

I hurried up the lane. The smoke curling from the kitchen chimney promised the still-welcome warmth of a wood fire. If I hurried through my chores, I would have time before dark to unearth my bag of marbles from the back of my closet. Tomorrow the ground should be just right for bunny-in-the-hole.

Fooling With Figures

My worst marks were in arithmetic.

"I have the wrong kind of brain," I told my mother, as she gazed with dissatisfaction at my report card. "It doesn't work fast enough."

This wasn't entirely true, since I had never given my gray matter a chance. Although mathematics would never be my forte, instead of doing it in my head, I was taking the easy way out — counting on my fingers.

"Practice makes perfect," said my mother. " You must spend more time on your homework."

But it was March, the winds were blowing fresh, skies were turning a special shade of blue, bannered with fleecy clouds. The burgeoning fetid smell of the earth held a promise. The hills and fields, free from the fetters of February, stretched endlessly, and I wore the winged slippers of childhood.

Evenings were for *Romance Isle*, Jack Benny and Fibber McGee and Molly on the radio while my mother taught me to crochet granny squares for her afghan.

Night after night I breezed through my homework, using my fingers instead of my memory, employing those same fingers the next day under my desktop to compute the classwork. My plan worked well until the teacher changed her tactics.

"Fourth grade come to the blackboard," said Miss Crosby, and the three of us, exchanging questioning glances, left our seats.

"Today you will do your arithmetic examples on the board," she said, and as we stood with the eyes of the whole classroom on our backs, she dictated the problems. How could I count on my fingers?

For almost half an hour our chalk squeaked away. My work was streaked with erasures and damp fingermarks. Maurice and Miriam finished their work and took their seats as I searched in vain through the gaps in my mental multiplication tables for the product of seven times seven.

When I finally sat down, my face burned with embarrassment as Miss Crosby corrected our work and pointed out my multiple errors.

Fixing me with her pointer, she said sternly, "You are to study your tables of sixes, sevens and eights and recite them before the class at the end of the week."

4

Undismayed, I stood at the front of the room on Friday, using the fingers on the side away from her desk as counters. Starting with "one times six is six," it was slow work but possible to add my way through the maze of numbers.

As I started on the multiplicands of seven, the class tattletale raised her hand.

"She's counting on her fingers," smirked Priss.

With a sigh, Miss Crosby told me to fold my hands in front of me and continue. I struggled my way through with some prompting.

My arithmetic marks never did improve. Next came long division and decimal fractions. Who could be interested in "What is the cost of 15¼ tons of coal at $8.40 per ton and $.50 for putting it in the bin" when outside the open windows smiled the long, bright sunny days of spring and a bloom was on the earth?

The Sunday Drivers

Tourists now seek the popular watering places along the coast or seclusion at lakes and ponds, but back when the motorcar was gaining in popularity, we had our own type of tourists — the Sunday drivers.

Located within easy driving distance from two large cities, we had an ample share of these patronizing and often predatory individuals, who drove leisurely along our usually traffic-free roads each Sunday afternoon. To them, the country was like a public park; without leave they acquisitioned the rocks from stone walls, picked pussy willows and lilacs and harvested apples along the roadsides. They walked obliviously through poison ivy, stumbled in their flimsy shoes, recoiled in horror from a bullfrog, and often used words I had never before heard.

Many of the back roads were still unpaved, and our long driveway looked like another road to somewhere. Cars would often drive in, find a dead-end beside the woodshed, turn around and go out, all the time staring and pointing at our quaint and rustic environment.

Late one Sunday afternoon, two ladies drove in, stopped where I was playing, and addressed me condescendingly.

"Little girl, dear, would you ask your daddy if we could take a picture of that cow?" asked the short plump lady with daisies on her hat.

I shook my head, puzzled. "I don't have a daddy."

The ladies looked at each other with a shocked expression.

"Then who is that man working over there?"

"That's my father," I answered.

"Oh," the taller lady simpered, "then will you ask *him*?"

I frowned. "I'm not allowed to bother my father when he's working in the field."

They exchanged another look.

"Well, then," continued tall and persistent, "would you let us take a picture of that cow with our Brownie?"

Again mystified, I looked around for a dog. "Brownie?" I asked.

"Our camera, dear. Could we?"

Just then the animal in question heard the hired man in the barn preparing for feeding time. Tossing ample horns, it began to canter toward the gate.

"It's a bull," I said.

6

Hastily the ladies jumped in their car and slammed the doors. Safely inside, they looked me over once more, my shock of tousled hair, faded cotton playsuit, bare feet, and homemade bandage on my knee where I had slashed it on the barbed-wire fence.

"That poor little soul," I heard the driver say.

I reported the incident to my mother, who sniffed loudly and crocheted a little faster. Before another Sunday rolled around, she had painted a sign that said "Private Drive" and nailed it to a tree near the mailbox.

I thought the sign added a touch of elegance to our modest farm, but I missed meeting those Sunday drivers. Being "a poor little soul" struck my fancy.

Cereal Souvenirs

Saturdays in spring were a time to be up and outdoors. The brooks were running free, interesting rocks had surfaced in the sandpit and birds were building their nests.

The fusty fragrance of April, unlike any other aroma, was discernible even through the seams of the old window frames in my bedroom, the putty so dried out the glass rattled in the slightest breeze.

Down in the kitchen, I was almost out the door when my mother stopped me for breakfast.

"There isn't time," I pleaded. "I want to get my chores done so I can play."

"Just some cold cereal, then," said my mother. "You know you have to have something in your stomach."

She was always placatingly apologetic but firm about making me eat. According to the school nurse, I was 20 pounds underweight.

"I can't eat it," I said, staring at the contents of my Peter Rabbit bowl. "There's a piece of rope in it."

With a sigh, my mother deigned a look. Sure enough, a small piece of deteriorated brown rope was floating in the milk.

"Well, I declare," said my mother. "You just can't trust these newfangled products."

Two weeks later a man knocked at the front door. We never used that door, but we could see he was a stranger and looked important, so my mother took the key off the nail beside the window and let him in.

"I'm from the cereal company," he said, after he shook hands with my mother. "We have your letter here about the foreign object allegedly found in one of our cereal boxes." He produced a handwritten sheet of lined paper. "Did you write this?"

"Well, yes," said my mother. "I thought you ought to know about the rope in case there's some in another box. If somebody swallowed it, it could be dangerous."

The man, who said his name was Mr. Ingersoll, looked pained, as though he had swallowed a cherry pit.

"Is this the piece of rope you maintain was in the box?" he asked.

"Yes, if that's the piece I sent you," answered my mother.

Emboldened by sitting in the seldom-used parlor, I spoke out.

"One of our sheep ate a piece of rope from the hay bale and died," I said.

Mr. Ingersoll looked even more discomfited.

"We are prepared to offer you a free case of cereal if you will sign this paper absolving our company of any further liability," he said.

"I just wanted you to know," repeated my mother. "There's no further liability as I know of, because she never ate it."

"Would you sign this then?" He moved to the edge of the horsehair chair.

"My husband told me never to sign anything," said my mother firmly, with a steely look from her eyes that indicated the interview was over.

"Then you plan further action?" asked the man.

"I don't plan anything," said my mother, "except to get my bread in the oven before noon."

Mr. Ingersoll looked puzzled and relieved. He apologized for the "error of the foreign object," said he was sure it would never happen again, and hoped we would continue to enjoy their products.

From the backseat of his car he carried in a carton containing 12 boxes of cereal flakes.

"With our compliments," he said.

I could see my mother was pleased with this windfall. "He sure made a fuss over one little piece of rope," she said.

For weeks, I voluntarily took time to eat breakfast on Saturdays, eating my way through the large supply of cereal. I was watching for another "foreign object," which never appeared.

"Foreign" to me meant the pictures of oddly dressed people in my geography book, and next time I hoped to find a pearl from Madras, India, or a piece of Chinese jade.

The Pet Show

Education was slowly changing. The original "three R's" had been incremented to include history, geography and English, as well as several minor subjects such as health, music and art. The hick'ry stick had long since given way to a short length of rattan, administered only on the palm of the outstretched hand.

One year when we went back to school after spring vacation, our teacher, Miss Crosby, acted as though she had taken a new lease on life, carrying on like a filly just let out to pasture.

On the blackboard, she had drawn with colored chalk a spring scene depicting trees, flowers, birds and even fairies. Against the back wall were placed a couple of chairs and a desk with a few library books on it. This was a "reading corner," she said, and when daily assignments were finished, pupils could go there to "make good use of their free time."

We exchanged glances of astonishment at this unheard-of departure from our regimented routine. But there was more and better to come — we were to have a pet show.

Uncharacteristically, Miss Crosby shared with us the reason for these changes. Having attended a seminar called Creative Learning, she was in the process of enriching our curriculum through cultural reinforcement and meaningful experiences.

We would each be required to write a short essay describing our pet, to be read aloud, and graded for content, spelling and punctuation.

On the day of the show, the schoolhouse was in a rumpus.

Prowling the room were three cats, a kitten, two dogs and Skinny's pet raccoon. Outside in the coatroom, my lamb, Sonny, was bleating in high dudgeon. Priss had brought a caged canary; two of the cats followed its every movement with voracious eyes.

The dogs were put outside, the raccoon settled inside the wood box, Sonny quieted down, and we read our essays.

As usual, Maurice's contribution livened things up.

"My father won't let me have no pet," he read. "Last summer I had a bullfrog hid in the barn for awhile, but when I took it to the pond for water, it got away. A bullfrog is green and black, can jump high and you can eat its back legs."

Miss Crosby shuddered and called on Charles, who took his place beside her desk and read: "The mouse is small and pink when it is born, then it turns gray. It eats most anything. I found this mouse in a nest in the corncrib. His name is Herman."

He took a matchbox from his pocket and slid back the cover. As the mouse jumped nimbly onto Miss Crosby's desk, she leaped from her seat with a stifled scream.

Alerted, the cats sprang into action, chasing Herman into the storage closet with Charles in pursuit. Outside the window, the dogs began to bark. The pet show had ended under a cloud.

Herman was never seen again, but for the rest of the year, Miss Crosby refused to enter the closet, sending a student emissary for needed supplies.

The chalk picture, grown dim and bleary, was finally erased, but Miss Crosby's creative classroom had not been a total loss. The reading corner remained, serving a definite purpose for motivation and improving our minds. Too, the pet show (though never repeated) emerged as an unparalleled course of events.

The old schoolhouse, derelict and deserted, its doorstep overgrown, still sits by the road, like Whittier's "ragged beggar sleeping." Passing by, I often think of Herman's descendants making their home there, undisturbed in the barren room where once resounded the voices of childhood.

The Sand Pile

Late every spring, when my father could spare the time, a load of sand was dumped under the big elm in the side yard, a huge sand pile just for us, to play in all summer long.

In the old Ford dump truck, he and the hired man would drive to the big sandpit a mile or so out of the village and shovel the truck half-full.

Such things were never discussed beforehand — my first inkling that today would be the day was the whiny sound of the dumping mechanism, followed by the heavy plop of the sand as it landed squarely where last year's heap had sat.

The first jump onto the pile was like a leap into summer. The sand, dug from the bowels of the pit, was cold and damp. It seemed to breathe as it settled into the ground, dappled with patterns of sun and shade from the branches overhead.

It was the best kind of sand, filled with large lumps of clay. Squeezed when damp, it would make a ball; it held its shape for tunnels and produced perfect "cakes."

From the shed, I brought the dusty box of Tootsietoy trucks and cars, discarded kitchen utensils and salvaged tin cans.

My friend Miriam came to play in the sand, adding her toys to the collection. She brought with her a "new boy," Rodney, who had moved into one of the tumble-down summer camps nearby. He had just one toy, a pale-blue motorcycle complete with sidecar and driver.

It was chipped and dented, missing one tire. It was also exactly like the one my mother had brought me the week before on her monthly trip to the city.

Rodney was hard to get along with — highballing the cycle over our neatly scraped roads and flattening our trees made of twigs.

After he left, I found my shiny new motorcycle missing from the sand garage where I had parked it. In its place was Rodney's beat-up model.

I poured out my indignation to my mother.

"Don't tell me," she said, "Tell him."

I combed my hair at the kitchen bureau, washed the sand from my bare feet and set off, clutching the offending toy.

At the cottage door, I hesitated. The gloomy silence under the tall pines was forbidding. One of the doorsteps had rotted in, and from under the battered porch, a scraggly cat peered at me with yellow eyes.

Timidly I knocked. The door was opened by a tall women, a jeweled comb in her long black hair, wearing a red dress and high-heeled shoes.

A gypsy! I thought with quailing heart. As I took a step backward, she smiled. Oh, well, I reasoned, in for a penny, in for a pound. I held out the motorcycle.

"Rodney left this at my house," I quavered, unable to go on with the rest of the story.

She thanked me, and as I watched dumbfounded, she leaned back against the doorframe and lit a cigarette. I had never seen a woman smoke. It's worse than a gypsy, I thought, she's a fallen woman!

Out of my depth, I turned and ran. The next time Rodney came to play I gave him a good kick in the shins and took my motorcycle back.

"You're a thief," I said, "your father should give you a good whipping."

"I don't have no father," he said. "He flew the coop long ago."

Once again I was speechless. All summer I broad-heartedly let Rodney play with the new cycle. I wasn't too surprised or chagrined when he took it with him when they moved away.

By the end of summer, when the squash vines had dried out and birds were gathering in flocks, the sand pile had magically melted away, its purpose served. Leveled by wind, washed away in the rain and flattened by hours of happy playtime, the sand pile had lost its enchantment.

The Flower Contest

By June 1, the school's wildflower contest was in full swing.

The child who brought in the first blossom of each species of a native wildflower received a point. The student who garnered the most points was awarded a prize, a small rectangular "flower book" with pictures in full color.

The flower contest fitted perfectly with our environment. The woods, fields and brooks were our stomping grounds, a natural conservatory of botanical specimens.

A girl usually won the contest. Many of the boys had lost interest after skunk cabbage was prohibited. This purplish, cowl-shaped herb was struck from the roll the year Miss Crosby found several redolent specimens on her desk, the room reeking with their obnoxious odor.

Morning after morning we carried our fragile offerings, stems wrapped in damp paper, along the dusty, graveled road to school.

The lowly bluets, pale anemones and a whitish-gray stalk we called "Indian tobacco" were among the earliest. My fingers stained a deep orange color from its sap, I was the first to bring in the pearly bloodroot, with its heart-shaped, deeply lobed leaves.

Each day the jelly glass vases on our teacher's desk were filled with bloom; the pink of the lady's-slipper (which has since become an endangered species) set off by the white clusters of Solomon's seal was flanked by bright-yellow cowslips, and the handsome jack-in-the-pulpit in its striped cutaway, plucked from its bed along the brook.

The fragrance of sweet violets blended with the aroma of wild columbine with its red and white spurred petals. All these and dozens more found their way to Miss Crosby's desk to be identified, discussed and tallied up.

I was sure I had won when I discovered a bed of dogtooth violets, nodding purple heads along the marsh. But the same day, Priss brought in a pale lavender hepatica, making us tied for first place.

On the evening of the last day of the contest, in the woods behind the cemetery, I found a bed of lily-of-the-valley, the slender stalks bowed down with their small bell-like flowers.

"Lily of the valley is not a wild flower," said Miss Crosby, when I placed it on her desk. I explained where I had found it.

"It was over the wall behind the cemetery because that's where someone threw a plant years ago when they cleared off a grave," she said. "It was seeded in."

"But it was *growing* wild," I persisted.

She thought a minute and said, "It is just like the so-called wild dogs that are roaming around. They are actually domesticated dogs that have gone back to nature. Therefore, they are not actually "wild."

Old Crosseye's word was law. We had no telephone in the schoolroom to call an arbitrator, no other teachers or a principal to offer an opinion.

As I walked home from school that afternoon, I tried to conquer my disappointment. Maybe next year, I thought. I still had four grades to go, four more springs in the old schoolhouse.

At supper, I put old Crosseye's knowledge to the test.

"Miss Crosby says a wild dog is really a tame dog," I said.

My father snorted. "She meets up with one, she'll change her tune," he said.

My spirits lifted. The image of Miss Crosby's ample girth treed by a wild dog took some of the sting out of the lost flower contest.

LILY OF THE VALLEY

Dandelion Greens

There came a time when spring had set foot firmly upon the earth — the lawn greened over; the red-winged blackbirds busily building in the bulrushes; the peepers in full chorus after dark.

One such day, as surely as the cock crows at sunup, I would be sent, carrying a bushel basket and knife, to gather dandelion greens.

It was a tiresome chore; I longed to be over the hills and away, to follow the high-running brook, to steal through the new-budded trees of the forest. With dread, I dug the young shoots from the grass, knowing the bitter, boiled leaves would appear on the supper table for many nights to come.

My mother eagerly awaited the dandelion greens for many reasons. Along with cowslips, they were our first taste of fresh produce since last autumn's killing frost; they added to a winter-depleted larder at no cost; and to top it all off, they were a renowned spring tonic.

"They're a purgative, that's why they're bitter," she would say as she prepared them for the pot. "They wash out the poisons in the blood."

The young plants were not as bitter as the older; sometimes my mother would blanch the leaves first, then boil again in fresh water. She always added a generous piece of salt pork for flavor.

In the oval serving dish, though adorned with a dollop of butter and sprinkled with salt and pepper, the slippery green mass to my eyes lacked appeal.

Appetizing or not, I was served a fair portion and under stern scrutiny, I was expected to clean my plate.

My mother and father really enjoyed the greens' fresh, earthy flavor, each year agreeing there was nothing quite like "a good mess of dandelion greens." In retrospect, I admit there was something about eating those jagged-shaped, acrid leaves that gave one a good feeling — whether physiological, spiritual or both, it's hard to say. But back then, they were gall and wormwood to me. Night after night I choked them down, counting on dessert to take away the taste.

In spite of it all, the dandelion was dear to me. Through spring and summer the blossoms profusely carpeted the lawns and meadows, bright gold in the sunshine. While in bud, the heads were bent down as if to pray, raising up in jubilation only when ready to burst into bloom.

16

The dandelion was a child's flower, a gilded treasure to be plucked and presented as a wilting Mother's Day bouquet; to brighten a May basket; to while away the playtime hours.

The hollow milky stems could be fitted together to make a flowery neck chain or a bracelet. The stems, when split, would roll up into curls.

Maturing into an intricate, whitened ball, its feathered fruits were transported by the breeze on a parachute of gossamer filaments.

Carefully picking these delicate white heads, we would blow off the puff of down fuzz to see what time it was — all off meant your mother wanted you and it was time to go home.

In those long ago days the dandelion, a common weed, today the scourge of lawn fanciers, was heralded by young and old — gold stars in the dusty grass; green goodness for a winter-weary palate.

NARCISSUS

The Narcissus

Visits to relatives were a duty performed regularly in the early part of the century; it was a time when "calls" were a requisite on the long list of a woman's responsibilities.

Excitement ran high the first year I was considered old enough to go along. The prospect of a trip off the farm — perhaps actually past the boundary marker into a different town — was awesome.

Driving was new to my mother, but other cars on the road were few. Between us on the worn leather seat of the pickup sat a basket; the smell of the hot yeast rolls and rhubarb pie mingled with the truck-cab odors of cigar smoke, engine grease and, faintly, manure.

My mother too, I could tell, enjoyed our mission. The truck was seldom available; today at noon my father had given his sanction. His work, he said, would keep him "on the place" all afternoon.

"I'll go to Uncle John's and see how he fared the winter," decided my mother.

Old Uncle John's dwelling place was lonely even by 1930 standards. This trip, my first to his isolated farm, seemed a long, though pleasant journey.

The one-lane dirt road meandered through forests of pine and oak. Groves of birches swayed, white and sylphlike against the darker, taller trees. Huge elephant-ear fronds of overgrown skunk cabbage rose from mud-blackened bogs. Tumbling gray rock walls traveled with us on each side.

Uncle John's farm had gone to seed; the fields and pasture rampant with weeds and shrubs, the barn settling on its sills, decaying.

The house sat back on a gentle rise, the dooryard choked with bramble roses and spiderwort; its rotting gutters embraced by overgrown lilacs and wisteria vines. The only sign of life was a wisp of smoke rising from a crumbling chimney. Here lived a patriarch, lonesome and lost to the world.

Old Uncle John was bent and frail; his hair thin and white, blue eyes clouded. The big kitchen was very warm, stuffy and dim; little light filtered through the vine-clad windows. Yellowed newspapers were piled in the corner, on tables and chairs. From an alcove a grandfather's clock, far taller than I, ticked loudly.

"Say hello to your great-uncle," prompted my mother. Ducking a sketchy curtsy, quickly surrendering his hot, dry, papery hand, I sat gingerly on a spindle-legged, dusty black chair.

When at last my mother gave me permission to go out and

play, I made my way through the tightly closed back hall into the golden largess of a May countryside.

Across the road, through an opening in the wall, stood a deserted burial ground; a few small, once-white, lichened stones showed through the matted grass.

Beside it was a breathtaking sight — masses of tall, delicate, stately flowers, like Wordsworth's daffodils, "fluttering and dancing in the breeze, continuous as the stars that shine . . ." except they were white. Their crisp, lilylike foliage gave off a fragrance heady and sweet, perfuming the air all around.

A neglected spot, a blissful wilderness, its beauty scarce seen by human eye, this green and shady sepulchral place lay undisturbed save by the piping of a quail, the scurrying of small woodland animals.

Kneeling, I plucked the dampened stems with care, filling both hands with regal bunches of those early spring blossoms.

They were narcissus, my mother told me on the way home.

"I suppose someone planted a few on one of the graves and they spread," she said, as we reveled in the scent and lavish beauty of these flowers grown wild.

My mother, who had attended an academy where the schoolmaster had a propensity for Latin and Greek, went on to explain.

"The narcissus is named after a Greek river god's beautiful son who pined away for love and was transformed into a flower," she said. How well the story seemed to fit that secret garden!

In the ensuing years, my mother timed her visits to Uncle John coincidentally with the season of the narcissus; in May, bountiful sweet-smelling bouquets graced our sitting room, the parlor and my teacher's desk. Each year the vast flower bed, sheltered yet untended, was more abundant than the last.

* * *

I have not passed that way for two-score years; yet the fusty smell of time-worn newspapers or the measured tick of a tall clock stirs still the memory of that enchanted field of flowers, a glimpse of the glory that was Greece.

The Planting

The potato crop was one of my father's best; into his two well-drained potato fields went unstinting care and hard work, and nature seemed to smile on him as well. His potatoes — tender, mealy, delicious — were much sought after, winning blue ribbons at the county fair year after year.

Yielding often 300 bushels to the acre, these "spuds" undoubtedly supplied the revenue for many of the finer things in our life.

I can't remember the exact date that first spring I was old enough to help plant. Each year was different; there was no set time. The fields were changeable too, used in rotation.

My father planted early, plowing as soon as the ground was suitably dried, following the nudging of some innate or acquired wisdom; perhaps a little of both.

Our fields weren't the only ones being planted — several of the bigger boys would be absent off and on for the rest of the year. Their truancy was acceptable because they were needed on the farm. If a farmer had sons, he didn't have to pay a hired man.

That week, while I was in school, my father and Amos, our hired man, had plowed the fall-manured 2-acre field in lap furrows, gone over it with a disc harrow and a smoothing harrow.

A homemade "drill" was used to lay out the rows — a wooden appurtenance like a huge rake with teeth two feet apart — pulled by the mare, Fanny, drawing arrow-straight lines in the soft earth.

By Friday night, the field was ready, the weather propitious. We would plant tomorrow as planned, my father announced at supper, and I was sent early to bed.

Just before dawn, we began work. The 40 or so bushels of seed potatoes, more than half of them already cut into eyes the day before, had been stored in the cold darkness of the second cellar. The covered barrels were brought to the edge of the field where my mother sat on a strawberry crate under the old elm. She was the cutter.

Women were known to be better potato cutters than men; they were used to such work and had more patience.

My mother, her small paring knife honed to a thin keenness, could cut a bushel an hour. A rag tied around her forefinger for protection, she sliced the potatoes into pieces with one eye, sometimes two, leaving a good-sized piece of tuber. The chunks, dropped into bushel baskets, were covered and kept in deep shade.

Now and then, as was her habit, my mother would hum a

21

familiar tune — usually it was "Work for the Night Is Coming."

My father made the trenches, 4 inches deep, following the drills. From a makeshift shoulder bag fashioned from a burlap sack, I dropped a chunk of seed potato every 12 inches in the trench. Amos followed behind, covering them over. Later on, with the horse hoe, the seeds would be more deeply buried — light is harmful to new potatoes.

Long before the noon dinner hour the rows seemed endless, even though I was "spelled" by Amos every hour or so. The dirt was cool to my bare feet, but the sun was hot on winter-pale skin. The potato bag, refilled time after time, seemed to grow heavier; the strap chafed my shoulder.

From the big pines, two crows cawed their approval; robins and grackles hovered on the fringes, scooping up a harvest of exposed worms and insects. I envied their freedom; inwardly my spirit rebelled. But there was no question of shirking on the work laid out for me.

On those unmechanized farms of the '20s and '30s, each person and animal pulled his weight, stoically did his share. Since reaching the age of 5, my chores had become heavier each year.

For our nooning, my mother fried up boiled potatoes and thick slices of ham, sent me to the cellar for a jar of canned peaches and made a big pitcher of cold tea. The meal was topped off with juicy slabs of rhubarb pie. It seemed one of the best meals I had ever eaten.

We worked until almost dusk; the field was finished, the potatoes were "in." Bone-weary, I nodded sleepily over the cold supper.

When my father settled down with his newspaper in the sitting room, my mother put a tin tub in front of the fire, filling it with hot water from the reservoir in the big black stove and cold water from the pump in the iron sink.

The soft soap smelled good, the warm water soothed away the bruises and scratches, the aches and pains.

Before falling asleep, I thought of the huge field, laying silent in the pale moonlight, where thousands of potato eyes would soon begin to stir and sprout; break through the crumbly earth and day by day rise up into a waving sea of green, while little new potatoes formed and grew in the darkness below. In spite of the dirt, sweat and plodding weariness, there was a splendor in it.

For the first time, I understood the words of the framed motto, spoken by Theodore Roosevelt, that hung beside my father's roll-top desk:

"Far and away the best prize that life offers is the chance to work hard at work worth doing."

Mayflowers

When I was old enough, my mother took me with her to find the Mayflowers, trailing arbutus. On our farm they grew in only one known place, near the banks of a small pond well back in the woods.

The pond was called The Sheep Dip, so small and shallow it could be made medicinal by adding a gallon or two of a coal-tar distillation. The sheep were then herded through it one at a time to control ticks or lice after shearing.

My father used more modern methods, but the old name for the pond survived.

The trees weren't leafed out, and as we sat on a rock to rest, the rattle of bare branches was the only sound in the stillness of the forest. The snow had scarcely left the ground; a chill lingered in the air.

This was the first time I had seen The Sheep Dip. It had a dark, brackish look; no pond-life grew in it, no ripples stirred its murky visage. Without being told, I kept well back from its blackened brink.

My mother brushed away dead leaves in several places along the shore, at last uncovering the rusty, dull-green veined leaves creeping close to the ground, starred by small white flowers. We picked them carefully, preserving the roots, leaving many blossoms to reseed.

I carried them in a posy, the hairy, earth-dampness of the sturdy stems scratching against the palm of my hand. It was the feeling of spring, of something nebulous yet certain.

I understood why my mother made this yearly pilgrimage, which now would be mine as well.

In what I thought was our prettiest vase, a small cut-glass sugar bowl with two handles, the Mayflowers trailed in natural abandon over the sides, wafting their delicate fragrance from the place of honor on the dining room sideboard.

Despite our precautions, the Mayflowers are gone now, their tiny white faces no longer hidden under the forest floor. Winterkilled, perhaps, but more likely the victim of a human predator, who unlike my mother, cared little for the continuity of life.

23

The Paths of Glory

Memorial Day meant three things to the little girl — the somber excitement of marching in a parade; the reward of an ice-cream cup with a movie star's photo on the inside cover; and the traditional first swim of the year. She had been born not long after the Great War, could sing the battle songs, knew what the day was supposed to mean: remembering the dead.

She marched as a member of the Sunday school group; it was her third year of participation and this Decoration Day she would make the whole march, to both cemeteries. There were a new and old cemetery to be decorated. The former was only a quarter-mile from the starting point; here the smaller children dropped out.

To the old cemetery and back was nigh onto three miles, and it was a prideful thing when you were old enough to go all the way.

Wearing her best pongee dress with matching bloomers, an evergreen wreath on her right arm, carrying a bouquet of Solomon's-seal and then-unrestricted lady's-slippers, she did her best to keep time to the cadence of the drum corps.

The damp wreath prickled the delicate skin on the child's bird-boned wrist. The sun of late May heated the tarred road, the smell of creosote mingling with the fetid odor of the swamp, the scent of lilacs by the old cellar hole.

As she walked the child remembered the memorial service held in the church sanctuary just before the parade formed. A few words of the Gettysburg Address, traditionally delivered by an eighth-grade pupil from the village school, lingered in her mind, "for which they gave the last full measure of devotion."

For the first time, the words had meaning; probably this understanding had something to do with being able to march all the way. Your last full measure must be the final time you could give your best. After that you would be burnt out, injured or have died.

Then a man from the American Legion in full-dress uniform had told a story about a battle in the war when all hope was lost and the commander said "Every man for himself and God for us all." These were the kinds of words that stuck in your head, making you glad to be part of Memorial Day.

The small parade tramped along smartly, past the sandy brook where the sleek, speckled trout lurked under the bank's over-hang; beside fern-clad glades and the bog, its mud hidden by the gigantic elephant-ear leaves of the skunk cabbage.

The rusted iron gates to the small burial ground were open, the grass neatly mowed. This was the smallest cemetery, but there were a few flags placed over graves from several wars. The children's wreaths were slipped down over the flag to rest on the metal holder, the bouquets slipped into the center of the wreath. In the sepulchral silence, the rifles were fired.

A bird or two flew up in alarm from the shelter of nearby woods; nothing else stirred. Taps was played, the lonely echo sounded from afar, across the leaning, lichened gravestones.

To the music of a mournful dirge they marched away, to begin the long journey back to the village.

Gratefully the little girl perched on the broad railing of the Grange Hall porch to eat the chocolate and vanilla ice cream, licking off a photo of a lady movie star. Never having been to a moving picture, the glamorous creature was unknown to the child, but her older sister would know, and perhaps even trade a stick of Teaberry gum for it.

She was hot and tired. The ice cream was cold and sweet, a prelude to the feeling of bare skin under just a wool bathing suit, the joyful ache of the cold water in the lake.

Yet there was a reluctance to cast off the mantle of homage, a yearning to do something more, as though the spirits of those fallen heroes had touched her own.

The minister came and leaned on the railing beside her. He wasn't wearing his Sunday suit, but just a white shirt open at the neck and sort of baggy pants. Seeing him thus gave her courage to speak up.

"I wish I could let people know how much I think of our brave soldiers," she said, blushing at her unprecedented boldness.

The minister looked across at the sun-baked road leading to the cemetery, then at the little girl's scuffed sandals, dusty ankle socks and flushed cheeks.

With a gentle smile he said, "You just did."

Minding the Books

My childhood was bounded by a trio of public buildings — the schoolhouse, the church and the library. All three were as familiar as the sitting room at home, but the library offered the most freedom.

Here, the only rule was silence. If quiet enough, you could browse undisturbed for hours.

The library, when first I knew it, was a brand-new building, a memorial built of rosy brick with white wood trim, Cape Cod style.

The big outer door had a heavy brass latch, hard to open. The first umbrella stand I had ever seen stood in the little hallway.

In winter, heat came up through a big, square hot air register with enough power to blow your skirt up to your waist. The large reading and reference room had a fireplace, never used.

The children's books were in the first section of the unheated, cement-floored stacks. Then came the aisles of novels, the non-fiction, the detective stories. As you got older, you kept reading your way further forward, both literally and figuratively.

All the books in the stacks had been moved from the former small wooden library building. Many of them were so seldom used that when opened, tiny mites would scurry across the pages. These volumes had a peculiar musty odor, not unpleasant, a smell I came to accept as "bookish."

The newer books and best sellers were kept on shelves in the main room, along with the librarian's big golden oak desk. The "bad" books were kept under her desk, signed out only to matrons in good standing.

The library was open only on Wednesday afternoons and Saturday mornings, and even with these limited hours was seldom well-patronized.

Week by week, year after year, I read through all the books in the children's section, taking out again and again old favorites like *A Little Maid of Bunker Hill, Bomba,* the *Jungle Boy,* envying him his machete, *Arlo,* and *Emily of New Moon.* Their familiar bindings seemed to welcome me like old friends.

Just as Anne, of Green Gables, longed to look like someone else, I yearned to look like Anne, with green eyes and red hair. Her attempt at changing hair color was so disastrous, I never tried it. Neither could I convince my mother to let my hair grow long enough to wear braids like Anne's.

Twice a month I could go from school to spend the rest of the afternoon at the library while my mother attended the ladies society meeting in the church next door. On the stepstool provided for the higher reaches, I would sit among the chilly open shelves, sampling book after book, pausing in thought to watch the sunset cast shadows on the hills or listen to sleet rattle against the windows.

The librarian was an older lady, tall, thin and implacably stern. Her saving grace was her absorption in her work — often she would forget I was there, relaxing her surveillance.

Then I could surreptitiously pore over the forbidden book of World War I photos, scarcely apprehending the horror so graphically depicted, or study the puzzling anatomy section (also banned) in the set of illustrated encyclopedias.

Tiptoeing up the iron spiral staircase to the attic under the eaves, I would gaze in fascination at a huge, hairy black widow spider or the butterfly collection in a glass case.

Though I yearned for them, I owned few books, but here at my fingertips were hundreds of volumes filled with the wisdom of the world — or so I thought. A good part of my early education in those impressionable years came from between shabby book covers.

It was a world seen through rose-colored glasses, the milieu of *The Bobbsey Twins, A Girl of the Limberlost*, of Grace Livingston Hill, the poetry of Robert Louis Stevenson, Edgar Guest and Mrs. Hemans. It was a society of romance and adventure, where the men consistently had a clean-cut profile, ladies had pale hands and a pure heart, and the world was well lost for love.

That era has vanished in time, but traces still linger in every small-town library. If you look hard enough, you may even find a well-worn copy of a book read long ago, pages from the past that awaken a pensive pulse of memory, long buried in more cosmopolitan layers of modern reading.

Speaking Day

As May edged toward June, the schoolroom activities turned more and more to cultural arts. With tin boxes of watercolors, we painted pictures of flowers plucked from the playground; rehearsed the choral compositions we would sing at graduation; memorized patriotic poems for the Memorial Day service.

The seventh- and eighth-graders, the only students who gave orations at graduation ceremonies, were writing and rehearsing their speeches.

Speaking Day was for sixth-grade pupils only; undoubtedly a preview performance in preparation for the all-important commencement a couple of years down the road.

We were allowed to choose for our Speaking Day recitation any selection from the anthology *101 Famous Poems*.

Memorization wasn't required; we must copy the poem neatly on white lined paper, become familiar with its intricacies, and read it aloud in an articulate and euphonic manner consistent with the poet's original intention. To add to the drama, we were expected to wear a costume.

Our declamation was limited to five minutes — if the poem of our choice had too many stanzas, we could edit it at our discretion, always keeping the poet's flow of thought in mind.

This was a tall order, but we all rose to the occasion and the tattered copy of *Famous Poems* was pored over hour after hour.

Since Speaking Day was an entertainment for our teacher, Miss Crosby, as well as any mothers or members of the community who cared to attend, we were permitted to practice outside on the school steps.

Miss Crosby, along with the lecturer of the Grange and the minister's wife (all childless to eliminate any partiality) would be the judges.

Charles admitted he chose *Hiawatha's Childhood* because he loved to say the words "By the shores of Gitche Gumee, by the shining Big-Sea-Water," and "Daughter of the Moon Nokomis." He wore a homemade paper Indian headdress and carried a rubber tomahawk he won at the county fair.

Priss recited *Maud Muller*, an old straw hat perched on her golden curls, a rake in her hand, looking herself a picture "of simple beauty and rustic health." She left out the stanza that told of "graceful ankles bare and brown," because her mother deemed it to be improper for public speech.

Predictably, Maurice chose the goriest poem in the book, *O Captain! My Captain!* The jaunty sailor's hat he wore was at odds with his emphatic and repetitive rendering of "Where on the deck my captain lies, fallen cold and dead," causing the minister's wife to press her rose-water-dampened handkerchief to her brow.

Skinny chose *The Barefoot Boy.*

"You only chose it so you could go barefooted in school," accused Maurice. But Skinny demurred — the poem reminded him of his own self, he said, a flash of poetic insight brightening his thin, freckled face. "The verses are full of pickerel, frogs, moles, the pasture brook and climbing trees," he said.

I chose *The Highwayman,* receiving a wry smile from Miss Crosby, who had already accused me of harboring "a romantic, Byronic nature." My "French cocked-hat" was handmade of colored paper but the "bunch of lace at his throat" was my mother's best white jabot.

Charles won the book prize as the best elocutionist (not surprisingly, he became a politician in later life), but we all agreed our Speaking Day had been a great success; a schoolday's highlight to be long remembered.

In memory, two lines spoken in Skinny's maundering, reedy voice bring back thoughts of the simple pleasures, the single-hearted happiness of childhood long ago:

From my heart I give you joy,
I was once a barefoot boy.

School's Out

The last day of school was almost as exciting as the Memorial Day parade, but in a different way. There was no band at school. It was like the whole earth was filled with music; bird songs, rustling tall grass, shrilling tree toads, soft murmuring of the brook; all calling us to golden summer days.

It was melancholy, too; not like the sadness for the soldiers in the cemetery, yet still making your stomach feel queer and your heart give a little jump when we sang our last songs, standing beside the battered desks.

After lunch, Miss Crosby went to the old piano. She had it placed sideways so she could read the music and still keep her eye on us. We could see her sensibly shod foot pumping up and down on the pedal; she played with plenty of verve. Three of the white keys were stuck down, but Miss Crosby said they would be fixed over the summer.

We sang "Flow Gently, Sweet Afton," "Darling Nelly Gray," then a round to cheer us up, "Are You Sleeping?"

Last of all, we sang "The Graduation Song." The three eighth-grade graduates looked pensively out the open windows and we looked at them.

One of the girls was teary-eyed, and the two that were in love tried to hold hands; without missing a note, Old Crosseyes cast them a withering look and they stepped apart.

Our desks were empty, inkwells washed out, textbooks stacked along the wall beneath the blackboards.

As the big clock on the wall inched along toward 3 p.m., signaling the end of the school day and the school year, we sat at attention as we had been taught — back straight, chin high, hands folded, feet flat on the floor.

"I wish for you all a rewarding and restful summer," said our teacher.

It would hardly be restful for the older boys; they would work long and tedious hours on the farms. We weren't sure what our rewards might be either, but her words had a nice ring to them.

"Goodbye, Miss Crosby," we chorused.

Each of us had a lot to carry as we headed home; forgotten mittens, cold tea jars, handkerchiefs and old copybooks from our desks; discards from the cleaned-out supply closet.

Skinny stuffed his share of broken pieces of colored chalk into the pockets of his corduroy knickers. Taking off his clocked knee stockings and heavy brogans, he tied the shoelaces together and hung them around his neck so he could wade through the brook on his way home.

30

Starting tomorrow, we would all go barefoot for the entire summer, except on Sundays. Tomorrow, time would be measured by sunrise and sunset, by the calendar of little new potatoes, Golden Bantam corn, dog days and ripening hazelnuts.

We fled the schoolyard, skimming along the dusty road, past the meadow's edge thick with blue flags, pausing at the brook where drowsy dragonflies hovered above the silver-clear ripples. From a far field came the clack of a mowing machine as a farmer cut early hay.

In the age-old pattern of what seemed then a lifetime of slumberous summer days ahead, my chores would grow along with the crops — picking strawberries and raspberries, lugging out ears of corn by the armful; carrying pitchers of cold switchel to the hayfield.

The boundaries of childhood were the woods, meadows, grove and apple trees. My joys would be the cooling refreshments of a piece of ice from the ice wagon; the juicy sweetness of the first shortcake; the strike of a pickerel on my fishing line; a nest of baby mice in the corncrib; a swim each afternoon in the soft, faintly murky water of the pond.

One hot summer night my father was sure to bring home a quart of vanilla from the ice-cream stand in the village. My mother would get out her green Depression glass cereal bowls. Our feast was always savored on the side porch while fireflies flickered in the meadow below.

"How was your last day?" asked my mother, pausing in her bread-baking ritual to get me a glass of cold buttermilk.

"It was sad," I said, "but next year I'll sit in a different row and get to use ink."

She nodded her head and gave me an extra molasses cookie, signifying approval that my education was proceeding as expected.

"Tomorrow," she said, with significant emphasis, "we'll go up on the side hill and see how the lowbush blueberries are coming along."

And I knew the long summer had begun.

SUMMER

Summer Sundays

In the early part of the century the church played a big part in our lives. When my grandfather was a boy, the church was the governing body of the community, actually administering physical punishment for "sins of the body and spirit."

The strength of religious authority was strong still; church on Sunday morning was a matter of course, as ingrained in our daily lives as the barn chores or the household tasks. Every person in the community "able to be about" attended each week.

To children, church attendance was an ordeal to be borne with stoicism most of the year. But on those warm fragrant days of June, the meadows thick with flowers, the pond a rippling blue, we chafed against the bonds of religious edification.

Sunday school classes were held before church, because most of the teachers also sang in the choir. We had small blue notebooks — each week we were required to bring a picture cut from a newspaper or magazine. This illustration would be mounted in our notebook with Cico paste, a Bible verse or Beatitude laboriously printed underneath.

When the church bell began to toll, calling the parishioners to services, we would troop up the stairs from the vestry, pausing to breathe the sweet, fresh air coming in the open vestibule doors; watching with awe the deacon who rhythmically pulled the thick brown rope that soared up through the balcony, the attic and into the spire where hung the great iron bell.

The respite was short; the organ boomed out the prelude and we were shepherded into the uncushioned family pews with our parents.

Diversions were few — the hymns whose verses over the years we learned by heart; the rustling importance of the choir as they stood to sing; the passing of the collection plate into which we could drop our nickel.

The long sermon, to a child, was unintelligible; it would be many years before the "children's message" became part of the service. We were expected to sit quietly, careful not to bang the heels of our Sunday shoes against the pew; in trepidation lest we sneeze, cough or have to be "taken out."

My mother was sympathetic. I think she remembered when she was a restless little girl. As the minister droned on or called down fire and brimstone on our heads (depending on the temperament of the current pastor), my mother would get out her freshly ironed handkerchief, and rolling it in a special way, make two babies in a cradle. One Sunday she turned the handkerchief into a rag doll using her wedding ring, but the ring fell on the floor, causing stiff necks to turn and putting her in disgrace for the rest of the day. Other times, she would smuggle me a piece of horehound or a peppermint drop.

Years later, when Big Brother Bob Emery ardently promoted on his television program the poem titled *A Fly in Church*, it was obvious he had grown up in an environment such as mine.

Lacking a fly to crawl over the red, well-scrubbed neck of the black-suited man sitting in front of me, the best diversion I remember is the day the man who pumped the organ fell asleep.

This man, small and wiry, very old, sat behind a screen each Sunday and worked a big wooden handle which pumped air into the bellows of the organ.

That Sunday, a hot and airless day, I was aroused from my sermon-induced stupor by the welcome words:

"For our closing hymn we will sing 'In the Hour of Trial.' "

The organist pulled out a couple of stops, held his hands over the keys dramatically while he flexed his fingers, and plunged them down onto the keys. But nothing happened except a small squeak.

The minister cleared his throat and intoned again, in a louder voice directed toward the screen:

"For our closing hymn we will sing 'In the Hour of Trial.' "

Still nothing happened. One of the deacons left his pew and disappeared behind the screen. After some rustling noises and loud whispering, the organ began to wheeze and the service continued.

On sunny days, through the open windows I could hear the sound of autos and happy voices as the "heathens" (as my mother called them) headed for the beach along the state road which ran past the church.

Sunday dinner was always served promptly at 1 p.m.; the most lavish and elegant meal of the week. Often the minister and his wife were invited, and my sister and brother-in-law were always among us.

Not allowed to play games on Sunday, we went for walks to pick flowers or sat on the cool granite front steps, making "pansy families" and watching the occasional Sunday driver go by.

Those days of Sabbath peace that are no more, stand out in memory. Though at the time the "day of rest" seemed arduous, perhaps because of this quiet oasis, this renewal of spirit, we worked better all our after years.

Launching Out

The farm and village were my whole world. I could count on the fingers of one hand the number of times I had been farther than the town boundaries.

Since most of my friends were in the same corral, the annual Sunday school picnic was an event to equal today's trips to Disneyland.

Our wardrobes were updated for the picnic with a store-bought playsuit, or at the very least, a new pair of socks. A lunch was packed in an old wicker hamper — jelly sandwiches, hard-boiled eggs, homemade pickles and a whole coconut cake.

My mother as a Sunday school teacher went along on the bus. By departure time, she had the wash on the line, the beds made, the kitchen redded up and my father's lunch, with plenty of cold tea, stowed in the icebox.

For some reason known only to the organizers, the picnic was always held on a Monday, perhaps because some of Sunday's brotherly love might still be fresh in our minds.

A seldom-equaled feeling of excitement and anticipation rose within us as the old bus lurched out of the churchyard and turned north out of town. We chattered and sang, squabbled over the citronella, and stared out the windows at the unfamiliar landscape.

The park was about an hour away. As we rode into the dirt parking lot, we could see the pond glistening in the morning sun, the green of the playing field, the well-worn paths under the pines.

The smell of sun-drenched balsam needles rose to greet us as we ran for the rough-boarded wooden bathhouses to change into our bathing suits.

Pungent pine resin oozed from the knotholes in the walls. The floorboards, damp and gritty, smelled of disinfectant. Some of the girls had rubber bathing shoes and one had a pair of white water wings.

Blankets were spread on the grass in the shade. None of the chaperones went in swimming. My mother had never owned a bathing costume, and would have felt immodest to expose her bare limbs.

At lunchtime the Sunday school superintendent gave each child two pieces of scrip, good at the little store for a bottle of soda and an ice cream.

The tall glass bottles of Nehi, Hires and Moxie were packed standing tall in melting ice in a big zinc-lined wooden cooler with a drain hole in the bottom, where water trickled away through a hole in the plank floor.

I traded one ticket for a bottle of lemon and lime, which emerged dripping and cold. It was my first drink of soda pop, the taste surpassing my wildest expectations, sweeter even than the nectar of wild honeysuckle blossoms.

After lunch, sack and three-legged races were held, as well as ball-tossing and horseshoe pitching contests, with prizes for all.

There was time for a last swim before we dressed to go home, our wet bathing suits stored in the empty picnic hamper.

Sunburned, sandy and tired, we were content to sit quietly on the long ride home, comparing the movie stars' photos on our ice-cream cup covers, counting the bottle caps we had collected around the picnic grounds.

Dimly we perceived a larger universe now marked with our footprints, a world crisscrossed with myriad roads, all leading somewhere worth going.

The Brook

On the first hot summer mornings, free from school, the chores put off until later, I would race away to the brook. It seemed a long way then, across the barnyard, through the pasture gate, across the meadows thick with clover, daisies and blue-eyed grass.

A muddy path led through the tussocks to a single-board footbridge, mired in damp earth on one side, set in the solid floor of the pine grove on the other.

The brook began as it splashed down from the farm pond onto gray boulders. Deep and dark brown under the heavy-leaved trees, rippling golden in the sun, the brook meandered its way through our farmland, fretting the banks after a heavy rain, flowing gently in the baking heat of mid-summer.

Each twist and turn, eddy and surge of the stream was known to us, until it disappeared under the wire fence that marked the boundary of our land, following its effluence out of our realm, into the green depths of the coppice beyond.

The boats we had carved from random bits of pine could be launched just below the cascade, a pebble or two for passengers, a matchstick mast.

Along the banks we followed their precarious progress, through the lacy ferns, past a brown leaf floating, under the verdant grapevine bower, bobbing around "swift-current corner," swirling through small puffs of foam.

The moss was cool and prickly between our bare toes, the slimy mud easily washed off as we waded on the pebbly bottom in the sunny shallows, where darning needles with blue-jointed bodies hovered silently on mica-thin wings.

Brown trout lay hidden in the watery caves along the banks or in the murky darkness under gnarled tree roots. Nearby, in the middle of their silver webs, yellow and black field spiders hung motionless, tree toads shrilled in the noonday heat.

At evening, the brook was a place for dreaming. The swallows skimmed swiftly over the water, the soft breeze of the dying day stirred the rustling water reeds.

Fireflies flickered as the night dew fell and bats swooped from the barn loft. The brook gurgled softly as the darkness deepened and the first star came out.

My mother, a welcome figure in the shadows, loomed at the pasture gate.

"Where does the brook go?" I asked.

"It joins a small river that flows into a big river running to the ocean," she answered, shepherding me into the house.

Just before bedtime, she carried a lamp into the parlor and took a thick green book with gold-edged leaves from the glass-fronted oak bookcase.

With rough, berry-stained fingers she turned the fragile pages and began to read. As the words of Tennyson's *The Brook* flowed musically through the room, I sat entranced.

The words of the closing verse echoed in memory as I climbed the stairs:

"And out again I curve and flow
To join the brimming river,
For men may come and men may go,
But I go on forever."

At the Seaside

For the inland dweller, a first visit to the seashore was one of the more impressive events of a lifetime. In the presence of the ocean, it is said, no one can endure for long unchanged, the sight, the sound and the mystery quickening the pulse, remaining forever locked in memory.

Of course I knew the ocean was there, a vast puddle of blue verging the New England states on the colored map in our geography book. Columbus sailed it; we sang "A Capital Ship for an Ocean Trip"; the fishman extolled his fillets as "fresh from the salt water."

When a very little girl still wearing thin, embroidered dresses and white kid shoes, the wind would often turn fresh and chill as I sat on the grass with my dolls or followed the croquet balls around the lawn.

"It's a sea turn," my mother would say, and scurry in the house for sweaters.

I pictured the frigid sea turning back from the shores of the far Azores and coming our way, like the horses turned at the end of a field row.

All my conglomerate ill-matched notions about the ocean were either confirmed or shot down the year I was considered old enough to go along with my mother on the Ladies Society picnic.

"Old enough" meant a child had learned to be seen and not heard; that she or he wouldn't infringe on the pleasure and relaxation of the adults.

It seemed a very long ride to the shore. Few women drove then; our Ford sedan was full. Wedged in the back seat between two well-endowed ladies, I could see little, but the side curtains were rolled up, the summer breeze soft and warm.

When the radiator began to steam, we stopped for water at a farmhouse close by the graveled road.

The picnic was held each year at a cottage owned by the president of the society. As we pulled up beside it, there was the ocean, vast, blue and green, moving, tossing, crashing on the sand, murmuring, splashing.

Some of the ladies went inside the tiny cottage to make a huge kettle of chowder; others settled in rockers on the open porch to talk and gaze at the infinite horizon.

Few youngsters attended; most of the members' children were grown and scattered. Sternly admonished not to go out of sight or in the water beyond our ankles, we skimmed with sandpipers along the hard sand, ankle-deep in foam, curling wavelets, discovering smooth-lipped shells, brown banners of slippery seaweed, a desiccated crab, satin-washed bits of colored glass.

Quickly I filled my shortening can pail with treasures from the sea, settling down to build sandcastles with a rusty tin shovel my mother had unearthed from the woodshed.

Later, under supervision, we dog-paddled around in "the basin," a large saltwater pool formed by shifting sands behind the cottages. Bathing suits were donned and shed in the small, bare-raftered bedrooms upstairs, where generations of sandy feet had worn smooth the wooden floorboards.

The ride home seemed shorter; more silent.

Skin glowing with a deeper tinge from the sun- wet radiance; the taste of salt on my lips; the smell of briny kelp rising from the sandy pail at my feet; washed in the wonders of the deep; I felt the sea was the best place in the world.

Mulberry Haven

If you had a mulberry tree when you were growing up, you had a friend. The thick, rough, deeply striated bark on the tree's chunky trunk made just-right toeholds for climbing.

A forking-out of the branches not far from the ground made an ideal sitting place in the broad lap of a well-hidden sturdy limb, where you could rest on its strength.

Here the squirrels carried their plunder from the square-nut tree. Higher up, the yellow-shafted flicker nested in the cavity of a dead branch among the shiny heart-oval leaves, anticipating the harvest to come. A deep hollow in the cracked base of the old tree gave off the sweetish odor of decayed nutshells and long-rotted berries.

The white berries began to ripen in July, closely packed clusters with tiny black centers, somewhat resembling a small blackberry, though different in structure.

The fruit, bland and almost tasteless, fell in a squishy carpet on the trampled field grass. Even though our between-meal snacks were only what nature offered, we ate few of the cloying mulberries. A time or two, my mother made mulberry wine, but of course I never got to taste it.

"Not a patch on elderberry wine," pronounced my father, as he drained a jelly glassful.

Our large and ancient mulberry tree stood to the north of the house — far enough away to be a haven, yet within sight and sound of the homeplace. Many a poem was composed there. In a tin snuffbox I had hidden in a hollow limb, were the stub of a pencil and the cut-up pages of last month's calendar for note-paper.

As I looked abroad from my rustling perch, the old tree cast its spell, seeming almost to whisper to me. Planted as a windbreak, I was told, the origin may have dated back to a long ago time when early settlers introduced the trees to New England in an attempt to start a lucrative silk industry.

The mature three-lobed leaves were fed to silk-producing caterpillars kept in the attic. After the silkworm eats the mulberry leaves, it spins a cocoon of fine silk fabric. The idea failed for various reasons.

Our graceful, drooping tree had become naturalized to its surroundings. In later years, the mulberry tree would be prized for its ornamental beauty and its faculty for attracting birds to the garden. Ours was considered a derelict on a farm where things were valued only for their usefulness.

The tree's long-forgotten origins stirred my senses as I sat in its boughs on sultry summer evenings. I mused that the tree's ringed heart yearned for its homeland of 5,000 years, the snow-capped mountains of China. It leaned, bending to one side, as though to look beyond the barn to the far East.

The birds ceased their evening songs, a sickle of a moon slowly brightened in the southern sky. In the gentle west wind of a New England sunset, the tree stirred beneath me — a lasting monument to departed hopes, a familiar friend from a faraway land.

The Thunderstorm

There were only two things my mother feared on the farm — the big black bull and lightning storms. With sensible precautions, the bull could be avoided. The lightning was devastatingly inescapable.

When the northwestern horizon darkened ominously and faint grumblings of thunder could be heard, my mother's dexterous hands became awkward as she hurriedly straightened up the kitchen.

"We'll sit awhile," she would say, her lips forced into a humorous smile as the thunder boomed closer. "Won't that be nice?"

Since "sitting awhile" in the middle of a summer afternoon was unheard of, I knew we were in for a real humdinger of a storm.

Over and over I had heard stories and tall tales of electrical storms and what the powerful force of lightning could do "anytime it had a mind to." A farmer carrying a pitchfork from the hayfield had been struck and killed; a horse seeking shelter under a tree had been knocked senseless.

Our house sat on a low rise, its chimneys topped only by the spreading elms. For years my mother had campaigned for lightning rods, which conducted the electric rays safely into the earth. My father had agreed to have the rods installed on both house and barn as soon as he could see his way clear.

Our farm was not many miles from a large river. The storms seemed to follow this waterway; we were in their destructive path.

My mother sat in the big Morris chair in what she had determined to be the safest place in the house — the corner by the china closet on an inside wall, as far as we could get from any windows.

I remembered the oft-told story of the bolt of lightning which came in a farmhouse bedroom window, flashed into the closet and skidded a leather slipper across the room, stunning the man in bed with its blinding glow.

Torn between a morbid desire to see such a fascinating phenomenon and trepidation lest such an event should actually occur, I teetered on the edge of a petit-point stool.

I was restless, but no, my mother said, I couldn't work on my sampler because of the needle which had been known to attract lightning. Of course I couldn't cut paper dolls because of the scissors. Neither could my mother use her crochet hook or pare the potatoes for supper. The kitchen, with its pots and pans, utensils and faucets was the most dangerous of all the rooms. Touching any object made of metal during an electrical storm was to risk the direst results.

My mother held rigidly to all the known rules and pitfalls for thunderstorms. Try as she would for my benefit to disguise her unbounded fear, its aura hung about us like a cloud with an electricity all its own.

I found the lightning fascinating to watch. "Like your grandfather," my mother said. "He stood in the open barn doors and watched it. It's a wonder he lived as long as he did."

The thunder crashed, reverberated, rolled along the earth like a giant hollow boulder, rattling the dishes, enclosing us in its deafening roar.

"When you hear the thunder crash, you know the danger of that bolt of lightning is past," said my mother.

"If you don't hear it, I guess you've been struck," I reasoned, but my mother said this was no time to tempt the devil with smart talk.

Zigzag lightning shot in a line of brilliant light to the horizon, breaking into a number of jagged forks and branches; sheet lightning fell around us like a blanket of flame. Windblown gusts of heavy rain pelted the darkening windowpanes.

When the lightning and thunder became almost simultaneous, I knew the danger was very close. An interval of six seconds between the lightning flash and the clap of thunder meant the storm's center was only about a mile away.

Suddenly a bolt went down very close by, the thunderclap so loud my mother jumped for her chair. It had struck near us, she said.

***

As the storm rumbled far away to the east, we stood in the yard among the downed branches, the crumpled leaves. Wading in the warm, muddy puddles I followed my mother down the lane through the cleansed, serene air to an awesome sight — a huge pine had been struck, riven through its heart by a ball of lightning, its mass of green branches fallen across the pond.

The acrid smell of brimstone hung over the mutilated tree. In wonder, I put my bare foot on the white wood of the trunk, exposed like naked flesh where the bark was torn away, the cracks weeping with tears of crystal sap.

A living giant had died here; I had learned firsthand the havoc nature could wreak.

One day, retrieving my jacks ball from behind the Morris chair, I noticed the back was held up by an adjustable metal rod. I never told my mother, figuring if the chair had survived this long, it was as good a place as any to be. Besides, I didn't want the location changed. I rather looked forward to the countless future storm-sit-out sessions in the security of our secluded corner.

Fragments of the Fourth

It never rained on the Fourth of July. The sky was always the deepest blue, the white puffy clouds piled high on the horizon drifted, silent and slow.

Every year, very early in the morning, my brother-in-law set off a huge cannon cracker, his 5-inch salute to the day. We strung the big American flag from the attic window to the elm tree across the yard, where it hung motionless in the summer heat.

The big paper bag of fireworks sat in the front hall, far away from the kitchen stove. My father had picked them out the day before on his daily trip to the farmers' market in the city

Fireworks dealers would open up in an empty store for a week or two each year, decorating the storefronts with red, white and blue bunting, flags and hastily painted signs. Their fascinating, exotic, and often deadly merchandise was displayed in chicken-wire compartments and boxes of sawdust.

My father chose well. There were pack after pack of small firecrackers, wrapped tightly in red or green tissue paper with colorful Chinese labels; packages of tiny "lady crackers," laced together; torpedoes, tightly glued balls of paper that exploded when thrown on a hard surface; Roman candles, rockets; boxes of sparklers.

.Novelties were different each year; a house on fire, or a revolving pinwheel to be nailed to a tree and lighted. A new silver cap gun with dozens of rolls of caps would last long after the holiday was over.

At that first big bang, our dog, Buster, slunk into the back of the woodshed, where he spent the day. The cats silently disappeared. There was no real holiday on the farm, so my father was at work in the fields, my mother in the kitchen. My friend and I had the dooryard to ourselves as we lit our pieces of punk and shot off firecrackers in every innovative way we could think of.

In the late morning, I was called to help shell the peck basket of peas. Any farmer worth his salt had peas by the Fourth of July, and ours were still dew-wet from the morning picking, opening with a pop. We sat on the shady grass under the elms, eating raw all the "culls," the tiny sweet-tasting peas too small to cook.

At noon, we sat down to a special dinner, eaten in the dining room to escape the heat of the wood cookstove. It was a feast like no other — the peas cooked with a piece of salt pork, the mess of little new potatoes dug just for that one meal; the huge chunk of delicate-orange-colored salmon, steamed in a piece of cheesecloth to hold its shape; huge pitchers of tea made with icy-cold well water. The dessert was strawberry shortcake made with baking powder biscuits.

In the afternoon, a parade on Main Street brought out the whole town, either as participants or viewers. Elaborately trimmed floats with ingenious motifs were often pulled by a yoke of oxen or a team of horses. Led by a local band, the floats were interspersed by marching units, decorated bicycles and pony carts.

As dusk fell, the old flag was pulled in the window, the older folks settled down on the cool granite of the front steps, and the night fireworks display was set off. Rockets careened out over the farm pond. Roman candles thumped their colored fireballs high into the air.

As the last sparkler lost its glitter and sputtered out, the pitch-darkness settled around us. We left the warm night shadows, sweet with the scent of summer gardens, to the stars in their solemn flight; the throb of the tree toads; the tiny sparks of the fireflies over the meadows.

Crossing the Delaware

The Fourth of July holiday seemed wedged far into the depths of summer; there was deep grass, deep shade, deep-blue sky. The water level in the well had shrunk; the hayfield was knee-deep in daisies.

My father believed in the Fourth of July, more than any other holiday, even Christmas. Each year he brought home from the city big paper bags filled with snap crackers, pinwheels, rockets, Roman candles and sparklers for my sister and me.

He planned the planting so we always had garden peas and new potatoes to go with the melt-in-your-mouth pinkness of the steamed salmon.

Most time-consuming of all, he volunteered to build a float for the parade.

Parades were very popular in the years before and after the turn of the century. Folks back then were starved for color and pageantry, fanfare and cadence. Creativity, stifled by the tiring drudgery of work on the farm, burst into resplendent life in the form of ingenious floats and flamboyant costumes for the Independence Day parade.

Materials were easy to come by; attics, sheds, barns and cellars were filled with odds and ends of every kind. In those days there were no yard sales, no flea markets, and nothing, not even a foot-long piece of string or a brown paper bag, was thrown away.

The best float I remember was built by my father and a few other members of some club or organization; perhaps the Grange, the Gun Club or the Junior Order.

These men spent many evenings back behind the house, hammering, laughing and joking. Each morning I would run out to check on their progress as the float took shape. The actual theme of the float was a closely guarded secret, so as not to detract from the impact of the parade itself.

They were building a huge boat, maybe 25 feet long, the rough boards covered smoothly over in black tarpaper, the silver shingle nails forming neat patterns. The impressive craft sat looking out of place among the apple trees in landlocked glory, like the alewives that came upriver and got caught above the dam.

The parade had so many participants, I wonder now who was left to be the spectators.

A band of some kind was hired from the city. Bands were very much in demand that day each year, so we usually ended up with a trio of bagpipers. To us, they filled the bill. Their colorful, authentic Scottish attire made up for their lack of musical volume.

Behind the band came the veterans, the flags, decorated doll carriages, our one fire truck and float after float.

The Ladies Society entry that year was a two-seater buggy completely covered in real pink and white roses with a bride inside, tossing out rose petals. It was pulled by a white horse wearing a collar of red roses.

My father's float was mounted on two sets of old dumpcart wheels and pulled by our span of oxen.

It turned out to be a depiction of Washington Crossing the Delaware. My father, standing proudly erect, supposedly peering back at the British army on the receding shore, wore a tricorn hat, a fancy uniform frock coat, knee breeches and black boots.

All around him in the boat, raggedly dressed soldiers sat on crates and boxes, or stood in the bow and stern with flintlock muskets at the ready. A large banner stretched across the side quoted Paine's words, "The Times That Try Men's Souls." It was an impressive sight.

After the parade disbanded, I was allowed to ride home in the boat. Its one moment of glory past, the historic craft was back once again among the apple trees.

Still, its mission was far from over. For the rest of the summer and fall, until my father dismantled it just before snow fell, my friends and I played in the boat. To us it became a pirate ship, a whaler, a gunboat. It broadened our horizons to unlimited heights as we sailed the seven seas, slew dragons and were smote amain, there among the quietly grazing sheep, the somnolent bees, the whirring grasshoppers.

The Fourth of July parades, like Washington's boat, disappeared without a trace. Independence Day became a holiday for going to the beach, to a carnival, a bonfire or public fireworks; for picnics, wienie roasts and fried clams.

Sampling these new diversions as I grew older was enjoyable. But somehow around the beginning of July, I would yearn for the skirling of bagpipes, the acrid, powdery smell of a string of lady crackers; the sight of a work-weary farmer portraying the Father of Our Country, crossing the Delaware in a homemade boat.

Memories on Ice

My grandfather's farm was bigger than my father's, and it was older. It had an icehouse, a small 2½-half-story building painted red to match the barn.

On hot summer days, while our mothers scraped their way up and down the rows of the strawberry bed to earn 3 cents a quart, my friend and I roamed the outbuildings and kept out of sight lest we be conscripted for picking. We were almost big enough to lend a hand, and "out of sight, out of mind" seemed safest.

There were no windows in the icehouse, just a little slot for ventilation near the roof, and the walls were double-thick with a dead space between.

When the dusty haymows became too hot for jumping, the icehouse beckoned. In June, it was still full almost to the top — we had to scale a built-in ladder to slip in through the wooden half-door near the roof, being careful to close it behind us as we dropped down into the almost complete darkness onto the huge cakes of ice submerged in sawdust.

The coldness of the ice through the damp, grainy, pine-scented sawdust was an experience both too heady and too chilling to bear for long, but also a feeling to be savored again and again, never to be forgotten.

In the fall, or perhaps sooner if we weren't frugal, the icehouse would be empty, transformed to a state just like any other building, where you could open the downstairs door and walk in. Many years later it was used as a garage, which seemed to me a mundane fate for so romantic a structure — a building that held a crystalized pond stored in its embrace for half a year.

The ice was lifted out with huge two-handled tongs and transported. Our ice chest was in the back shed, where my father had built a platform to hold it and the messy drip pan beneath it, always overflowing. With typical Yankee ingenuity, he had fastened two or three leather strips to the wall to hold the sharp-pointed ice picks, small and large.

Opening the door of the ice chest with its corrugated zinc lining, and "picking" off a sliver of ice, made too much noise to get away with it very often. The ice was precious; it took the place of the cold pantry and kept the food fresher for longer periods.

The ice box was progressive, but far from perfect. The ice often melted before the next cake arrived. I can still remember the taste of rancid butter, but on the bright side, we often feasted on sour milk chocolate cake.

When the ice wagon began its round, the men of the family gave up the icehouse. Cutting and storing the ice in February was bone-chilling, backbreaking, dangerous work.

The ice wagon would come clattering up the driveway in the stillness of a hot country morning, the tongs hung on the back rattling away. It was noisy, especially if the ice cakes shifted in the slippery enclosed interior.

When the jovial iceman opened the double doors, we felt the flow of damp, cold air as we reached for broken-off chips. If it was an extra-sultry day, he would often chip us off a good-sized sliver to savor in the shade long after he rumbled away.

He wore a vest with a padded leather back, and with the tongs would effortlessly heave the huge cake onto his shoulder, carry it to the shed and slip it in the top compartment of the chest.

Like the milkman, the ragman and the fish man, the iceman was a familiar figure in our lives, and the most welcome. He was to us the equivalent of today's ice-cream truck. His accompanying clinking and clanking were as effective in pricking up our ears as any modern bell, and his shards of crystal-clear ice, flavored only by nature, were our first Popsicles.

Making Hay

Our hay crop was one of the most valuable harvests; by far the largest in acreage; the most necessary for the economical operation of the farm.

Hayfields had to be cut each year; an unmowed field, in just a couple of summers, became an incipient forest as trees and bushes found a footing. Hayfields lost on land left vacant by death or taxes could never be reclaimed.

Hay has an optimum time for harvesting; the clover in half-bloom, the timothy at full.

The crows woke me at dawn with their raucous cawing. The sun was rising in a clear blue sky, the dew would quickly burn away. The weather promised fair— it was haying time.

My father rode the horse-drawn mowing machine; the hired man's scythe dropped the high grass into ordered rows around the edges of the field, along the walls, in the small cul-de-sacs where the horse couldn't turn.

The long grass was left to lie where it fell, to be dried by the heat of the sun and the gentle west wind. Later it would be raked into long windrows for further curing.

The hay rake was just that; a huge iron rake with arced, sharp-pointed teeth suspended between two large wheels. A foot pedal and hand lever raised and lowered the teeth.

Fanny, the mare, harnessed to the wooden shafts of the rake, stood patiently at the edge of the field.

The mowing machine was a cruel leveler. Blossoms fell; rabbits scampered, scarcely spared by the chattering, razor-keen blades. Birds flew up in a flutter of fright, their hidden nests bared to the merciless glare of the sun, to the eyes of predators.

The day became a sea of dust, tiny seeds whirling, the acrid smell of horse and dying weeds. In the hottest hour, I carried a pitcher of cold switchel and a tin cup into the field, averting my eyes from a green snake impaled on the cutting blades. As the men paused in their work, my father yielded to my pleading and allowed I could take the rake once around the field.

The scoop-shaped perforated iron seat was far too large for me; I had to stretch to reach the pedals. The horse was no problem, it was an old story and easy apples for her. She plodded along with a minimum of guidance, sweat lathering up under the harness strap on her haunches, black tail swishing rhythmically at flies.

Hat in hand to let the breeze riffle his graying hair, my father watched me laconically for a few minutes before waving me back. I didn't know it then, but he was sizing me up to run the hay rake the next summer, when my legs would be longer, my stamina strengthened.

Perched high on my vantage point, I reined in the horse and gazed across the vastness of newly mown meadows and fields, shorn of much of their beauty, but fragrant with the sweetness of fresh-cut, drying grass. The huge blue dome of the sky stretched into infinity; a lightning-struck dead tree stood starkly on the far horizon, like a warning sentinel at the very gates of the unknown, faraway forest.

Both the horses were hitched to the big wagon to get the hay off the fields and under cover in the barn. My father swung me up on top of each load, to trample it down and make room for more. The hay was moved by pitchforks into the mows; the last load of the day was rolled triumphantly through the big double doors and left to sit on the wagon.

Back in the meadow, although the birds would not return, the moles and mice would be reweaving their intricate paths through the stubble; the glossy grackles feasting on seeds and homeless insects. The snake's severed tail would quiver spasmodically until the set of sun.

That winter, each time I forked down hay to Fanny and Buddy, I talked to them.

"This may be the hay I raked up for you," I said.

But they only went on grinding up the fragrant forage with their huge yellow teeth, shifting their cumbersome iron-shod hoofs, pensively gazing out the tiny, diamond-shaped windows of the manger at the meadows they had mowed, raked and harvested.

Going Berrying

Wild blueberry picking used to be a serious business. It was woman's work, one of her yearly round of fundamental seasonal tasks, to pick and preserve enough berries to last through the year. After that, according to longstanding tradition, she could sell the rest for "pin money."

My mother planned on 24 pints for preserving, and about 12 quarts for fresh blueberry pies and steamed blueberry puddings in season. With that amount behind her, she could earn money for "gimcracks," as they were called by my father — new curtains, paint, oilcloth for the kitchen table, cosmetics, or perhaps even a new hat.

"Going berrying" was often an all-day affair; blueberries come and go very quickly. Many expeditions also took place in the long evenings after an early supper.

My mother always dressed for the occasion in an old pair of my father's pants, too big and held up by suspenders; a faded denim "jumper," and battered felt hat.

Come July, the woods were hot, but arms and legs needed protection from the hordes of mosquitoes, as well as from the onslaught of sharp branches and thorny vines in the forest. The hat offered shelter from the sun; if the heat became unbearable, she would line it with grape or oak leaves.

She looked like a tramp, as did her similarly dressed companions. Cotton housedresses and aprons cast aside, they obviously enjoyed the necessary masquerade, a welcome departure from the humdrum existence of life on the farm.

It was highbush blueberries she was after as soon as they ripened — they were larger and far easier to pick than the earlier crop of low-bush. There were acres of head-high bushes, full-laden with their tiny blue globules, the fat of the land, free for the picking.

These hardy bushes, the product of more than 100 years of growing and reseeding, were scattered in profusion on the hillsides, in the valleys, through the rocky brush-grown pastures.

Two or three women, and in the evening an occasional man, went together on these trips, for safety as well as social reasons. Packs of wild dogs still roamed New England, and bona fide tramps were a commonplace sight. Out of sight and sound of civilization, a sprained ankle could present a serious problem to the solitary rambler.

There was much gossiping and calling back and forth. If silence fell, it meant a picker had found a "good bush" (loaded with extra-large berries) and wanted to keep it for herself.

Familiar landmarks were seen year after year — the row of black walnut trees on the ridge, the pile of rocks by a spring, the copse where we saw the deer at dusk, a well-worn cow path. We shared this domain, and the berries, with the birds — the shy hermit thrush with his low, sweet flutelike song; the gurgling liquid "kook-a-ree" of the red-winged blackbird; the three-note whistle of the brown thrasher from his conspicuous treetop perch.

The lowbush blueberry crop had come earlier in the month. Often in the late afternoon I would be called from play to pick a cup or two to make a blueberry cake for supper

Kneeling, I would inch along in the berry patch at the edge of the woods, eating as I picked. It began as drudgery, but as the tiny berries covered the bottom of my kettle and began to mount up, I always felt a stirring of satisfaction, an ages-old pride in putting food on the table.

Lips, knees and fingers stained purple, I carried my small harvest to the hot, steamy kitchen, where my mother picked them over, washed and dredged them with flour before they disappeared into the thick yellow batter in the big yellow bowl.

Blueberry Bounty

As soon as I was old enough to walk nimble-footed through the woods, my mother took me berrying. Undoubtedly my babyhood and ensuing years when I had to be "left" with this or that neighbor had kept her foraging excursions to the barest minimum.

We always went in the morning; other household tasks had to wait 'til afternoon during blueberry-picking season, which was an integral part of our unwritten nature's calendar.

The munificent blueberry harvest, free for the taking, was essential to round out our often limited larder. For a few weeks we would feast on blueberry muffins, blueberry pie and blueberry "biscuit," a tender, cakelike batter bread to be eaten with butter.

My mother also put up about two or three dozen pints for the preserve shelf in the cellar; the rest of what she picked was her money crop. Women in those days were expected to earn the money for personal gewgaws and household luxuries like oilcloth, cretonne and household enamel. There was always a ready market for blueberries, and 30 cents a quart was coveted remuneration.

It must have rained at times during blueberry season, but I remember day after day of pure blue sky, deepening heat, breathless humidity.

Those first years, my mother would insist that I pick at least a cupful, partly as discipline, I suppose, but mainly as a dictum of the unspoken farm philosophy that each person and animal contribute a fair share.

There were several blueberry pastures on our holdings; we would pick them all. Setting out at an early hour, the woods were cool as my mother guided us along the gloomy wood-road through the depths of spruce, oak and birch to the vast expanse of low, scrubby bushes showing blue in the strong sunlight. Places that had been logged long ago or burned out in a forest fire made the best blueberry patches.

The birds fluttered and twittered over the morning's supply of insects. Rabbit trails led off into the brush. Pheasants or quail, alarmed by the rattle of our buckets and cans, flew up with a beat of wings. Once a gray owl, fallen asleep on his night watch, soared off in grandeur at our approach.

My mother, a born picker, was in her element; berries mounted steadily in her big shortening can. Each time it was full she emptied it into the 10-quart water pail. Now and then she sat back on her heels to take off her cloth hat and wipe the sweat from her forehead.

Ours was a companionable silence; the few words we spoke only intensified the brooding quiet of the countryside.

My required cup of plunder safely stored in the big bucket, I was free to eat my fill of the dusky, blue globules, chase butterflies or sit in the shade at the edge of the field, whittling a pine twig with my jackknife or making cloud pictures in the white puffy thunderheads piling up on the horizon.

Back in the yard, my mother would measure out her berries — a colander full for the day's cooking, the rest in wooden quart boxes for market. On canning days, they would all go into the preserving kettle.

For lunch there would be hot blueberry biscuits to go along with the salt pork in cream gravy and beet greens. Dessert for supper would be steamed blueberry pudding.

The next morning we would set off again.

Most exciting to me was the pasture far from the homeplace, offering new territory to explore. Here my father would drop us off, returning just before noon.

My mother could judge by the sun when it was time to "pick towards the road." Soon we would hear faintly the truck horn, still a good ways away, signaling my father's approach. He didn't take much to waiting.

Carefully we would climb over the stone wall with our morning's yield, like lost travelers emerging from the jungle.

Sitting on the tailboard of the rattly little green pickup truck, bare feet dangling just above the dust, lips stained purple, I thought about the abandoned bird's nest I had found, the hollow tree that hummed with bees, the perfect birch for swinging.

Never did I become a true-blue devoted picker like my mother, but as the years went by, the hours spent in the blueberry patches of those sun-struck summertime woodlands brought me the money to buy copybooks, ink, a goodly supply of Schrafft's candy bars and my first jar of Lady Esther face cream. Who could ask for more?

Haying Time

August came, bringing the apex of summer heat and long summer day after sultry day with few storms. It was haying weather.

My father watched all the weather signs like "Mackerel sky at night, sailor's delight," and the way the wind was blowing. He listened to E.B. Rideout from the radio on the kitchen shelf, as he gave his weather forecast from "Eastport to Sandy Hook." Picking just the right days was crucial for getting in a good crop, and there was no second chance.

Haying time meant work for every member of the family. The meadows and fields, sweet with tall grass and clover, stretched like a rippling, green ocean to the woodlands edge, where the fronds of ferns blended their faint fragrance with the scent of hemlocks and pines.

Scythes had been honed on the grindstone to a razor sharpness, along with the blades in the lethal cutting bar of the mowing machine with its single iron seat.

The first day was for cutting, as the mare pulled the mower back and forth across the fields. Where the machine couldn't be navigated — along the stone walls, in the lower meadow close to the brook, or on the steepest knolls — the extra hands, hired by the day, swung their scythes in perfect arcs, felling the summer's growth. Baby rabbits, flushed from their hidden nests, would scurry to escape the merciless blades as they clacked back and forth.

I couldn't help but admire my older sister, who drove the many-tined hay rake, guiding old Billy and pulling the heavy lever that lifted the sharp tines, leaving a neat roll of fragrant fodder.

A big trestle table would be carried out under the shade of the elms in the side yard, and on this my mother would set out the noonday dinner. It was usually platters of fried ham and potatoes, hot biscuits with jam and lots of cold tea to wash it down.

The haying went on until the first stars came out, to get all the hay cut and laid out for drying, while my father kept his weather-eye cocked at the thunderheads piled on the horizon.

My job each day was to lug the big yellow pitcher of haymaker's switchel, along with a tin cup, out to the field in midafternoon. The sharp, newly cut stubble was too hard on bare feet, so I would strap on my two-buckle sandals and set off.

I was seldom allowed into the "man's world" of the farm, and did my best to appear strong and dependable as I struggled to keep my frosty pitcher upright while I dealt with flying grasshoppers, mosquitoes, and an occasional snake. The men would smack their lips and smile at me as they drank in turn, but I could see how they made sheep's eyes at my sister.

Once our regular hired man, who my father said was missing some of his buttons but who was always kind to me, gave me a brown thrasher's nest with four gray and brown spotted eggs in it. He said the mother bird never would come back, now that the nest's hiding place had been "tore up."

Haymaker's switchel was made of well water, molasses and vinegar, with a chunk of ice from the icehouse floating on top. It was the most thirst-quenching drink available. The ingredients also kept a man going.

When the hay was dry, the hayricks would be driven out to bring in load after load, filling the dim lofts to the rafters. My mother used a huge rake with wooden teeth to pull together what the pitchforks missed, and as I scooped up those small windrows in my arms, I often thought of a hungry horse or sheep making a meal of it some cold winter's day.

The last load was always the best, as we rode in regal style on top of the well-built load, through the big doors into the barn.

Sunburned browner than ever, our legs and arms scratched and prickly, we would wash at the pump in the kitchen sink, hardly able to stay awake to eat the late supper of cold potatoes and canned salmon.

My father raised his eyes and looked around the table at us.

"You done good," he said. It was bad grammar — we knew it, and he knew it, but that was his way, and a word of praise from my father was as sweet as the smell of the new mown hay, safely laid up in the old red barn.

A Man's World

It suited me to be a tomboy growing up, except now and then when certain ladies threw disapproving glances my way. This usually happened when I was seen sitting on the carriage shed roof behind the church, or when we bolted out of Sunday school class the instant the bell rang.

"Be more ladylike," our teacher would chide, but the call of the open fields was too strong.

My mother tried hard to make me into a silk purse. She tied big bows of ribbon on my straight Dutch-cut hair, sewed strips of lace on my dresses, and gave me a green enameled comb, brush and mirror set for my birthday.

I didn't mind any of these things, but other considerations were just more important.

The housewifely pursuits forced upon me did go against the grain, such as ironing to perfection the two dozen or so men's and ladies handkerchiefs each Tuesday, or wearing my best dress when we had company, smiling demurely as I passed the teacakes.

"Well, here's your little girl, growing like a weed," they would say, meaning I was too tall for my age as well as my dress and thin as a rail.

Boys, it seemed to me, had all the luck. With their nifty knickers and knee stockings, they could wriggle through the brush, skin through a hole in a fence, or shinny up trees. When we played "Run, Sheep, Run" at recess, our voluminous dresses caught on the smallest branch or bunched up round our knees.

Boys could perform the most daring exploits, seldom getting caught and were in fact, *expected* to misbehave.

Then, too, they had pockets, deep recesses that could hold jackknives, marbles, blow-gun ammunition, candy, pieces of string or any number of useful objects. One boy had a dried frog's leg for a charm. As girls we were unequipped, and one year made small cloth bags to hang around our necks and carry our treasures.

"Boys will be boys," was the fondly spoken cover-up for all kinds of sins. We girls, on the other hand, were constantly warned to be "modest." This meant keeping our skirts pulled down and our stockings pulled up, even when making an especially tricky shot for "bunny-in-the-hole" or sliding into third base.

60

There was just one thing we didn't wish equal rights in — the rattan. This tough, flexible piece of a tropical palm tree was used on the boys as a punishment.

The culprit would be taken out into the hall, door closed. We could hear the whack of the rattan as it struck against the extended palm of the hand, the number of times depending on the seriousness of the crime. It struck fear in our hearts.

Few of the boys ever made a sound, but their eyes would be red with unshed tears as they returned, head down, to the classroom. Some of them could count on being licked at home if they were licked in school.

One day I was standing on the raised platform at the front of the schoolroom, a piece of gum I had been chewing stuck on my nose as punishment. An eighth-grade boy asked permission to "leave the room," and from my vantage point I watched as he strolled out behind the bathroom building. Soon small wisps of smoke began to rise from his corn-silk cigar.

"What is so interesting out the window, miss?" asked the teacher.

"Oh, nothing, ma'am," I said, pulling myself to respectful attention.

I would never tell, and suddenly, for no reason, I too was happy that "boys will be boys."

61

Gathering In

Autumn on the farm was a time of abundance, a season for humans, like the squirrels, to store up food for the long winter ahead. Time and the days were growing short, and nothing could be left to chance. Some morning not far off there would be a skim of ice on the farm pond.

Canning had been going on all summer and would continue until the last green tomato was made into piccalilli, but most of the work was outdoors.

On late fall afternoons after school and on Saturdays, I would be called on to help out with jobs equal to my size and strength. Catching squash was one of the most demanding, when I was middleman in a chain from the huge mound of squash to the truck.

At the pile, my father established the never-hesitating rhythm of an automaton as he tossed each squash into my waiting hands and I quickly turned and passed it to the hired man in the truck. There could be no pause to glance at a late butterfly or encroaching wasp.

From the painful experience of a sprained middle finger, I had cultivated unfailing concentration. "Treat them like eggs," said my father, as a bruised squash didn't keep well and was unfit for market.

I was middleman again when my father sawed wood. The saw shed had an open front, and all through the fall the big electric saw blade screamed its way through cord after cord of hardwood. As my father sawed, one person stood to "take away," while a third received the 16-inch stick and tossed it into the truck.

This, too, was tiring and demanding work, but had its own reward, a ride in the back of the truck deep into the wood lots to bring out another load of 6-foot lengths.

Here in the hushed silence, miles from the nearest house, were the seldom-seen brooks, the eerie cedar swamp, the deer paths. While the men loaded the truck, I could search for partridge berries or the rare adder's-tongue for my mother's berry bowls, collect tiny balsam cones or venture beyond the clearing into "the black forest."

Each year after a hard frost, my father would stop the truck on the way out, and with his bone-handled jackknife, cut a huge, twisted swag of red bittersweet bursting from its orange jackets. This glowing garland from the land of the forest would ride beside me in splendor on top of the load as the truck ground its way in low gear through the narrow, rutted wood road.

Picking up potatoes was a dirty, dusty chore. The wooden bushel boxes were driven out into the field and placed along the rows. My father could throw out a hill clean with a single motion of his four-tined fork, and hardly ever stuck a tuber. He could dig an acre in 10 or 12 hours, and we would fill 300 bushel from an acre in a good year.

Potatoes were our best crop, and the Burbanks, Green Mountains or Katahdins brought a good price in the October marketplace. Bushel after bushel were harvested and stored in the dark chill of the second cellar.

As the sharp coolness of night came down and the first twinkling star was pinned to the darkening sky, we moved toward the lighted kitchen windows and the certain comfort of a hot supper.

SMOOTH-LEAVED SUMACH

The Cornfield

By late August, the field of golden bantam sweet corn was a sea of living, rustling green, 9 feet tall, promising a bountiful harvest.

Venturing into this maze only a few steps, the world was lost from sight; nothing could be seen but dark green and purple jointed stalks, the long-pointed quivering leaves, the silk-crowned husks, the topped-out tassels high above pointing to the sky.

Once inside this featureless forest of corn, a child could lose its bearings, becoming completely lost, but following any straight and well-spaced row of stalks to its end would bring you safely out.

Deep into the cornfield, 20 rows down and 14 rows over, was a tiny clearing, where a couple of stalks had failed to grow. This was my "room" in the corn, a hushed hideaway seen only by the crows flying overhead.

Laboriously, my playmate and I each carried in a big rock for a seat. Here in this cultivated cave, secure in a wilderness of green, we feasted on ground falls of Seckel pears, ruddy early apples and baby carrots filched from the kitchen garden.

Secretly, day after day we skimmed through the cool aisles of lisping leaves, careful not to damage the towering plants, watchful to emerge unseen.

Picking time came. Wooden bushel boxes, some darkened with age, others still new, smelling of pine, were stacked at the edge of the field, the truck parked nearby.

My father was the picker, deftly twisting off each ear with a squeaky, juicy wrenching sound distinctive only to picking corn.

My sister and I were the carriers; outstretched arms piled to our chins with fulled-out, brown-silked ears, we plodded through the long rows, dumping our loads in a pile on the trampled grass at the edge of the field.

As my father moved deeper into the cornfield, our trips grew longer, the burdens heavier. The moist, sharp-pointed stalk-ends of the ears pressed painfully into the tender skin of our arms; the long coarse leaves reached out to brush our legs and faces as we passed, like hairy, dew-wet fingers, making us feel prickly all over.

Dust rose from the hot, powdery earth, coating our bare feet with grime as we made trip after trip in and out of the field.

Slowing down or dropping an ear brought a sharp reprimand; we kept up the pace as best we could.

My mother was the packer. The ears were put haphazardly in the bottom of each bushel; the top tier had to be packed just so in even rows, the big end of an ear placed alternately to the little end.

"Looks like a hundred bushel to the acre," said my father, well-pleased, as we washed up at the pump for nooning.

My sister and I exchanged glances of resignation; rain or shine, we would be carrying again the next morning.

For now, our labors were ended; we were never expected to work more than half a day.

During the afternoon my father would load the truck; each weekday morning at 4 he drove to the farmers' market in the city, returning with a roll of bills wadded together by an elastic band.

After picking, the cornfield, demolished of its harvest, stood in fading splendor until cut down with the mowing machine, gathered up and bundled into bulky shocks.

Traipsing over the stubbled acres, I found the site of my secret hideaway, identifiable only by the two flat rocks; it was gone, along with the rustling cornfield, as surely as the long golden days of summer.

I sat in the flattened field, the drudgery of "lugging out" forgotten. Only the golden goodness of the corn crop was remembered in the shocks that stood like rustic tents against the sky; the rows of filled glass jars on the preserve shelf in the cellar; the platters heaped high with milky, tender ears, dripping with butter, pepper and salt.

A sharp, chill breeze crept over the land; beside the meadow the dark brown velvet pompoms of the cattails set off the yellow fronds of dusty goldenrod. In the mirrorlike blackness of the farm pond a red maple leaf drifted. As blue as the sky above, a gentian curled its fringes; thistledown floated dreamily on the soft wild grape-scented air.

Nature was already tossing seeds to the winds for next year's growth, another season's harvest.

Back to School

Going back to school meant new leather shoes. My father would bring them home from the city.

They were always the right size, because he had drawn around my foot on a piece of paper before he left. I had a new middy dress, cut down from one my sister had outgrown, and my mother had trimmed my Buster Brown haircut.

It felt good to see the flag waving once again from the white flagpole in front of the school. Inside, the floor had been newly oiled and the wood stove polished.

The same old battered textbooks were piled on a table up front, with a few new ones mixed in. I hoped I might be lucky enough to get one of the new books, with untouched pages that fairly crackled and smelled like fresh paint.

Mothers never came to school, even on the first day. The new first-graders were sent off with an older brother or sister, or even a neighbor's child.

Skinny's 5-year-old sister, already seated in the very first row, was sobbing.

"You stop that caterwauling," said Skinny, "or I'll take you home."

"I *want* to go home," she wailed, and kept it up all through opening exercises.

Most of the girls had new dresses, but Annabella's was the cat's meow. It was pink, with a dropped waist, very tight, and actually showed her knees.

Annabella's mother, Violette, made all her clothes, copied from a ladies magazine call the *Delineator*.

Violette was a city girl, and my mother said she was a vamp and a coquette. I thought she was pretty with her white skin, tangled blonde curls and lip rouge.

We all had to go to the blackboard, alphabetically, and write our full name and grade. When Annabella wrote her name, her dress hiked up even further in the back. The boys all snickered and sighed, and Miss Crosby kept Annabella in her seat the rest of the day.

"What is so great about Annabella's skinny legs?" I wrote on a piece of paper. I folded the note and passed it to Marcella, but before her hand reached it, Maurice intercepted.

A few minutes later the note came back to my desk. "You are too yung to knoe," Maurice had written across the bottom.

Like a hawk descending on a wounded rabbit, Miss Crosby swooped down on me and snatched the note. After she read it, she delivered a 10-minute lecture on modesty, took away my recess, and sent Maurice to the corner.

Things were not going well, in spite of the fact that Miss Crosby had received two apples, a jar of beach plum jelly and two bouquets of garden flowers.

After lunch, she gave us an assignment that students have received since the year one — we were to write a 50-word essay on "What I did in my summer vacation."

She gave us 45 minutes to compose and transcribe these literary offerings. She went around to each of the upper-grades' desks, filled the inkwells from a big glass bottle and passed out wooden penholders with shiny new points.

"Watch your penmanship, grammar and spelling," she admonished, "but make your essay interesting. You will read them in front of the class."

I wrote about the Sunday school picnic and received a nod of approval.

Florence had taken a long motor trip of more than four hours to the seashore. "We brought back real lobsters," she read, "but the car broke down and they died. So we fed them to the pigs." We all laughed and she flounced to her seat.

Priss had gone to see a real play in an opera house, and Skinny had been to a Chatauqua.

Maurice was last.

"I cleaned out the barn cellar and shoveled manure for three days," he read from his crumpled and ink-blotted paper. "I didn't go no place, but one night my father took me hunting coons. I et too many green apples and got the horse colic. My Aunt Sarah dosed me up till I like to died." He rolled his eyes and clutched his stomach.

The room erupted into laughter, and outside the open window Skinny's dog began to bark. Miss Crosby banged her desk with a ruler so hard the petals fell off the asters.

After we quieted down, Priss tried to pour oil on the troubled waters. She raised her hand for permission to speak.

"What did you do in *your* vacation, Miss Crosby?" she asked in her best manner.

Miss Crosby patted her neatly coiled hair and stood a little straighter.

"I matriculated at the university," she said.

We didn't know what that meant, and fearing embarrassment, were afraid to ask. Chastened, we sat in silence until dismissal.

Miss Crosby had won the first round.

Another School Year

In the warm September air the flag hung limply on its white pole in front of the small school building, a signal that vacation was over, the halls of education open to us once more.

A silence had enshrouded the school all summer; deserted, it sat amid overgrown grass and flowering mullein plants. A wild morning glory vine wrapped the broken porch railing; tiny maple tree seedlings sprouted in the cracked wooden steps.

This was the day when shiny new shoes scuffed through the dusty dooryard, lunch pails clattered, a dozen shrill voices shattered the stillness. We circled the school grounds, making them once again our own.

Under the big oak, the cluster of rocks by the tumbled stone wall was still there, the ground carpeted to our delight in shiny, brown-capped acorns. This was our council chamber, the rocks our thrones, the hovering white birches our witnesses.

Giving the splintery wooden seesaws a bounce up and down, we ran through the lacy wild carrot field, trampling the soft grass of "the humps," our outdoor lunchroom. We scrambled through the abandoned gravel pit, our collection place for tiny white stones and mottled pebbles, and on to the thicket of scrub growth where the big boys had been caught smoking corn-silk cigarettes.

We paused by a tiny grave, its jackknife-carved wooden cross still standing. Here lay buried the bird that had somehow been locked in the schoolroom one spring night, beating itself to death on the windows trying to escape.

Our teacher stood on the porch; ceremoniously she lifted the big brass hand bell. Its strident clanging echoed to the edge of the woods, the pastures beyond, stilling the cawing crows, raising the heads of the sheep grazing across the road.

Inside, the wooden floor was newly oiled, some of the battered desks newly varnished. Unbroken pieces of chalk and well-clapped erasers lined up in the tray under the blackboard, where our teacher had drawn a picture in colored chalk — an apple tree with the falling apples spelling out "Welcome Back."

Miss Crosby's strict and strait-laced jurisdiction was tempered by perception and compassion.

To the smart aleck, the cheater, the breaker of rules, retribution was swift, often painful. Yet a child slumped over its desk, vainly trying to hide despondency or pain (we were raised to be spartan) roused Miss Crosby to gentle probing for the root of the misery — a baby sister was very sick; the mare was cast in its stall; the wild dogs had run a sheep to its death; a fox had ravaged a carelessly secured hencoop.

Miss Crosby cosseted these victims of life's inequities with sympathetic murmurings, pats on the head and a lightened work load.

With less empathy but fairly professional skill, she bandaged skinned knees, removed splinters and staunched bloody noses. For more serious medical crises, she dispatched a fleet-footed pupil to run the quarter-mile to the village store for aid.

Miss Crosby was the only adult in an isolated, ill-equipped building, responsible for a large group of contradistinctive children. We viewed her with respect — she could shovel snow; breathe up a fire from ashes; deal with a mad dog and repeat from memory the Preamble of the Constitution and the first two paragraphs of the Declaration of Independence. She was our instructor, our mentor, our Rock of Gibraltar; inspiring, cajoling, browbeating us through our primary education.

Now she sent off the oldest eighth-grade boy to knock down a wasp's nest in the girl's outhouse.

"Wasps don't do nothing this time of year," he grumbled, but Miss Crosby only corrected his grammar and told him an ounce of prevention was worth a pound of cure.

After confiscating a wad of gum, opening all the windows on the south side and removing a nectar-drugged bee from the bouquet on her desk, Miss Crosby began passing out the dog-eared textbooks.

From inside my desk, I slipped out the brand-new pencil box my mother had brought home from the city, the most wondrous thing I had ever owned. Under a snap-down cover, the compartmented top layer held three yellow lead pencils, a pink oblong eraser, a 6-inch wooden ruler and three crayons. Most wonderful of all was the little knobbed drawer underneath that contained a folded-up, colored map of the world.

The wall clock ticked loudly; across the aisle, Skinny was rolling spitballs. Miss Crosby struck a chord on the piano and we all stood up to sing "America."

Another school year had begun.

Summer's End

By the middle of September, we were well-settled into our school routine. Although slingshots and peashooters still bulged in the boy's pockets, the high spirits resulting from a long, undisciplined summer had been toned down.

Fall was late in coming the year our teacher decided to take us on a bird walk. Contrary to the calendar, the weather remained warm and sunny, as though reluctant to let the season pass.

The sky was a soft, melting blue, puffs of thistledown wafted lazily through the mellow air, the rich, ripe tints of the cornfields were set off by swathes of Queen Anne's lace and goldenrod. Surely the bird walk was just a means to an end.

Some sort of curriculum had been set up by the school board, but it allowed a lot of leeway. The bird walk would come under general science, we were told, and marks would go in the rank book.

"Funny time for a bird walk," said my mother, "when most of the birds have flown south." But parents back then never questioned what happened at school. Teachers were considered paragons of knowledge.

Miss Crosby pinned on her navy blue straw hat and led the way across the field behind the school, into the cool depths of the woods road. We saw two crows.

"What can you tell me about the crow?" asked Miss Crosby.

"One crow sorrow, two crows joy," I quoted. "It means we will have a happy day."

Maurice snorted. "Crows is varmints," he said. "Every spring my father shoots one and dangles it in the cornfield to scare the others away."

Miss Crosby shuddered. "That will do," she said sternly, and read us the page on crows from her little bird book.

We saw some mourning doves and learned they were known as devoted lovers in the bird world, always flying in pairs.

Skinny volunteered to go off the path into the underbrush and scare up some partridges or quail. He was gone so long Miss Crosby got worried, but we knew he was likely sitting on a log eating the licorice he had in his pocket.

On his return, he reported seeing a gray owl, but Old Crosseyes said it didn't count, because at least two people had to see a specimen to make it official.

After we added chickadees and blue jays to our list, Miss Crosby consulted the little gold watch she had pinned on her bosom, and we turned back.

The sun was high in the sky, the air perfumed with the scent of wild grapes. A chipmunk paused on the old stone wall before disappearing between the weathered gray rocks. Yellow butterflies hovered beside the sandy path.

Just as we reached the schoolyard, we heard a deep, resonant honking overhead. Looking up we saw a wedge of geese in striking formation, necks outstretched in powerful flight.

Summer was ending after all. A new season was creeping over the hills, rising from the meadows, stirring in the trees.

The splendor of autumn was yet to come, and like the migrating birds, we climbed the old wooden steps to new horizons, unknown challenges.

FALL

Fall of the Leaf

Fall came, with a tang in the air and color running riot in the woods, shades of russet, gold and bronze weaving a brocade of beauty over the hillsides and through the swamps. Could the sky really be so bright a vaulted blue, the trees so vividly brilliant?

Leaves that had rustled in unattainable billows of green high above all summer came tumbling down to lay their final glory in the dusty grass at our feet.

"Autumn comes after August," said our teacher, craftily combining a spelling principle with general science, as we began to study the patterns of fall.

We were disappointed to learn the panoply of trees clad in yellows and reds wasn't, after all, the work of Jack Frost with his paintbrush — it was all a matter of something called chlorophyll.

For homework, we carefully gathered the most colorful leaves we could find, each one seeming more gorgeous than the last.

"Just six each," she said, "the prettiest, best-shaped and most-perfect you can find."

On a misty, mellow morning, as the chattering swallows gathered for flight over the brown-stubbled fields, I set off for school with a half-dozen superb specimens securely stationed in tissue paper between the pages of my geography book. I had chosen five leaves from the rock maple, and one deep red spray of sumac, which I hoped would count as one.

Although the sun was still warm, the wood stove in the schoolroom was kindled with a low fire to take off the chill. Near the back of the stove sat an old aluminum kettle, half full of melting paraffin.

All morning we could smell the resinous wax as we went through our lessons. Projects were always done in the afternoon.

After lunch, the teacher called us to her desk one at a time, to approve our selections and give a short talk on the characteristics of the tree it came from. Open in front of her was a lavishly illustrated book called *Trees and Shrubs of the Northeast*.

When my turn came, she gave my first five leaves a nod of approbation, but recoiled in horror as I placed the spray of sumac on the golden oak surface of her desk.

"Not this!" she said, gingerly pushing my most splendid offering into the wastebasket with the tip of her ruler. "Don't you know sumac is poison?"

74

My face turned half as red as the leaves in question as the room erupted in laughter. I was allowed to go outside and find another leaf to make up my quota, but chosen in haste and chagrin, it came nowhere near being a match for the sumac.

At the work table, we dipped the leaves in the liquefied, crystalline paraffin and placed them on sheets of wax paper to dry, preserving for all time a few fragments of fall. Later we would mount them for display around the room.

That night at supper I asked my father if sumac was poison.

"Some is, some isn't," he said.

"My teacher said the red leaves I took from the bush down by the sheep gate were poison and would give a rash," I persisted.

"She's a city girl," he said, and that, of course, explained everything.

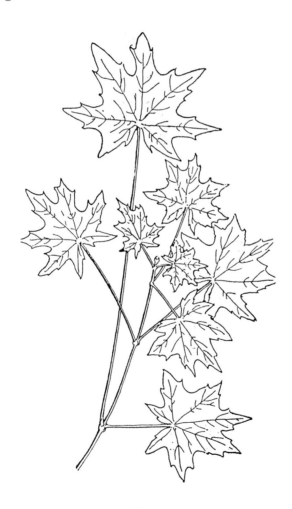

The School Superintendent

Once a year the school superintendent would visit our classroom. Economic conditions forced rural communities to band together as a district, hiring the best-qualified superintendent available, sharing the cost.

The burden of education was entirely borne by each small town individually; state aid was yet to come, and the federal government had little impact on our lives — its main thrust was in offering a topic of conversation as to "what them fellers in Washington is going to do next."

The school, though it made up the largest item in our town's budget, was still poorly maintained. Lighting came from the tall windows; heat from the wood stove. There had been talk of installing inside plumbing, but the water pail and outhouse were still in use.

The lack of creature comforts was not considered by the spartan members of the school committee to be as important as the quality of the education offered. Thus the "plumbing money" went to subsidize a superintendent.

There was an underlying distrust of this "outsider," but "book learning" was universally revered.

"He's an educated person, you know," was a phrase guaranteed to open any door and lay out the red carpet.

We sat quietly in our seats, readers open before us, subdued by the importance of the occasion. Not even Maurice tried to "pull anything" during the superintendent's visit.

The road scraper went by, pulled by two plodding horses, followed by a dumpcart filled with gravel. It was mud season. The wall clock ticked loudly in the barren room; clearly we heard the sound of an automobile, the slam of a door, the tramping of feet. Excitement and trepidation ran high.

From her desk, Miss Crosby greeted the superintendent, who loomed large among us. We noted with awe his fashionable salt-and-pepper suit with the folded white handkerchief in the breast pocket; his shiny brown shoes decorated with tiny perforations; his erect posture and pale, uncalloused hands.

I couldn't help but stare at the gleaming silver clasp holding his striped tie in place. It seemed the epitome of tastefulness, fashioned in the shape of a tiny, open book.

This model of learned gentility sat on the reading bench at the front of the room. Most of us, in honor of the impending visit, had been decked out in our best clothes. Miss Crosby had dressed her hair with unusual finesse, adding an extra comb at the back. She wore a new, white lace jabot. As always when a man appeared she was flustered and breathless, but this was considered normal for a maiden lady.

Old Crosseyes chose one pupil from each grade to read a suitable passage, and with some nervous stumbling this went off well. Another group was sent to the blackboard to do figures, and the upper grades performed in an oral (pre-rehearsed) history quiz.

At recess, while the superintendent conferred with Miss Crosby, we clustered around his 1929 Oldsmobile. To our disappointment, the rumble seat was closed, but Priss, who had actually ridden in one, described the padded leather seat, the rubber-matted floor, the thrill of riding along behind the driver at high speed.

Back in the classroom, we stood beside our desks and sang *The Ash Grove* before the superintendent took his leave.

He thanked us in a courtly manner and said goodbye. At a nod from our teacher, we chorused in unison "Goodbye, Mr. Baldwin."

Pleased with our deportment, Miss Crosby decreed an extra recess. Skinny and some of the other boys began making mud balls, throwing them against the back of the school where they landed with a satisfactory "thwack" against the white clapboards, forming a pattern of glistening brown stains.

It was the perfect ending for the superintendent's visit.

Facing the Music

When my girlfriends and I had turned 12, our mothers introduced us to what they termed "cultural advantages."

We fought against them. No longer could we run wild and free through the hills and pastures, or settle down in the spare room for a long, rainy afternoon with our extensive collections of paper dolls. Civilization was encroaching on our lives; we must conform.

We were enrolled in dancing school. My feet were squeezed into white Mary Janes with a shiny black button for the strap, over snowy-white ankle socks. My hair was tied with a pink ribbon to match the sash on my ruffled organdy dress. I felt awkward and foolish, even refusing on the first day to go into the Grange Hall, until I realized I felt more foolish sulking outside.

"Don't slouch," said my mother, "and smile, or the boys won't ask you to dance."

Little did she know. I didn't smile, but had to take a partner anyway. The teacher had cunningly planned the sessions with an even number of boys and girls, and no one was allowed to sit out.

The girls sat on folding wooden seats on one side of the polished dance floor. The boys, their hair slicked back with brilliantine and wearing long pants instead of knickers, sat on the other side.

The middle-aged teacher had a strong personality. She could bubble with enthusiasm under the malevolent glances of 12 pairs of eyes.

"Ladies and gentlemen," she burbled, "you are here to learn one of the cultural advantages that will stand you in good stead for the rest of your lives." We groaned inwardly. Outwardly, we kept politely deadpan faces.

The boys learned how to bow from the waist when requesting "the pleasure of this dance," and where not to place their hands while dancing.

The girls had it a lot harder. We learned how to rise gracefully, how to sit (legs *never* crossed). A lady, we were told, must not loll back in her chair, or even lean back against it. When walking across the dance floor we must not stride (as on a golf course); amble shoulders stooped, arms swinging; trot or shuffle. To our delight, she demonstrated each of these comportments. Above all we must never whisper, giggle, nudge each other or point.

We learned all these rules, but we also learned to dance. We mastered the waltz, the fox trot, and the Virginia reel. We tripped the light fantastic through broom dances, ladies choice and promenades. *One*, two, three, *one*, two, three counted our teacher, as we sorted out our feet and began to relax.

Our eighth-grade topics of conversation changed. Suddenly boys, our former playmates and tree-climbing rivals, became "cute," "smooth dancers," or "drips."

After eight weeks came the recital. The public was invited to attend, and it was a very popular affair, as our teacher supplied a three-piece orchestra. To our teacher's dismay, none of the families involved could afford a long, formal gown, but we all had new Sunday school dresses to wear.

We, her graduating students, were paired off for a grand march down the hall and back, then each couple, by turn, decorously danced the waltz around the floor to show their newly acquired skill. After that, there was general dancing for all. For the first time, the boys could choose a partner or not, just as they pleased, and we could refuse to dance if we wished. We were on our own.

I sat, knees close together, ankles primly crossed, my back straight and hands loosely clasped in my lap. Feeling like a toothpaste advertisement, I smiled and smiled. As I waited and prayed, I longed for big blue eyes, golden curls and no freckles. My mother was watching, my big sister was dancing with somebody handsome. What if I was a wallflower?

I felt like the proverbial spider; I had to catch a fly — in this case, a trousered companion — or be left in disgrace. Oh, to be belle of the ball!

"Remember," my mother had said when I asked to stay at home, "if you look as if you are having a good time, you *will* have a good time."

It seemed an eternity had passed, but actually the orchestra was only halfway through its first rendition when an older boy I had never before seen stopped in front of me and said casually, "May I have some of this?"

As we whirled around the floor I could smell the bay rum on his cheek and feel the scratchiness of his tweed jacket against my bare arm. He finally spoke. He was Prince Charming, but he didn't say I was a knockout or that I had beautiful eyes or gorgeous hair

"You can really dance," he said, as we twirled in perfect rhythm.

I forgot my toothpaste grin and gave him a real smile.

"So can you," I managed to answer, and breathed a sigh of pure happiness.

My first "cultural advantage" had paid off, and I was launched into society for sure.

October

October on the farm was everyone's favorite, a glorious month. Keats' "season of mists and mellow fruitfulness" was a bacchanalian feast to the eyes, the senses, the spirit; a time of laden vines, abundant sheaves, chockfull cellars. Over all was the feeling of a summer's job well done.

The work load was lessening; there were moments of leisure to savor the scent of sweet apples falling wild; to gather hazelnuts; to watch the gossamer milkweed seeds drift against the blue sky or the thistledown take to the breeze.

Barberries flamed up, vermilion, blood-red. Leaves, every shade of yellow, red and orange sifted silently through the soft air, a winter's blanket. Sumac flaunted crimson velvet heads.

We ate oyster stew, apple dumplings, Blue Hubbard squash, roast pheasant, wild grape jelly that had scarcely set.

The whirring blade in the saw shed screamed hour after hour, neatly slicing seasoned cordwood into stove lengths, spewing fragrant sawdust even into the pockets of my father's work jumper.

Bushel baskets of cranberries, like ruby jewels of the Nile, sat on the side porch, waiting for just the right winnowing wind.

The ladies society held its first fall meeting; play rehearsals began in the Grange Hall for *Leave it to Dad.*

Baked beans, brown bread spread with juicy, glistening salt pork and chunks of molasses-apple pie tasted extra good as white frost crept up out of the hollows, venturing across the fall-plowed fields.

Three white frosts, then a storm, said my father — the storm that would transform the world into the chill drabness of November.

But for now, the air was redolent with the smell of fragrant leaf smoke, decaying windfalls, drying foliage.

Acorns plopped steadily from the oaks edging the woods. Squirrels and chipmunks scurried back and forth over the old stone wall, flicking their tails. They were laying in a big store of nuts — it would be a hard winter. The corn husks had been thicker, too, a sure sign.

The elms were not as colorful, but our ancient maple near the edge of the pond stood majestically in a giant golden circle of its own fallen glory, sending on each gentle breeze crisp-curled leaves to float like fairy boats on the dark water.

Scuffing through the rustling leaves underfoot, I headed home from school, carrying my books by a strap. On the hazy horizon a black horse browsed over a still-green pasture. I scanned the sky for the wedge of geese, that one day soon, like an undulating brown arrow, would fly overhead.

Passing the newly erected telephone pole at the end of our lane, I remembered with pleasure that tonight I could listen to *Amos 'N Andy*. Just the past summer we had electricity installed, and my father had brought home a big brown table radio shaped like a church window.

A pile of pumpkins, small and round, tall and skinny, was stacked by the cellar bulkhead. For Halloween, I would have my pick.

My mother was in the woodshed dusting off a homemade bird feeder that had seen many winters. "With a nail here and there," she said, it would hold for another season her offerings of bread crusts, suet and cracked corn.

As the sun slanted low across the lawn and supper smells were filling the kitchen, my father drove in. From among the wood-chips, axes and bucksaws in the back of the truck, he lifted a heavy swag of bittersweet, orange and gold berries bursting from the gnarled and twisted branches. A cutting of this colorful vine, fresh from the cool depths of the cedar swamp, was his annual October offering.

Its autumn glory would blaze forth from the cut-glass bowl on the sideboard until Thanksgiving, long after the first gentle snowfall had covered the earth.

The Popcorn Tree

It took a good frost to bring the horse chestnuts tumbling down from their leafy hiding places. Near the schoolyard was one pyramidal horse chestnut tree, over 60 feet tall, casting its shade over a low stone wall, and offering its ornamental beauty to all who passed by.

In the spring, we called it "the popcorn tree" because of its showy white clusters of blossoms. These slowly grew into plump, leathery green capsules covered with sharp spines, each containing a large, brown, highly polished chestnut.

On nippy October mornings, scarcely could we wait for recess to gather these treasures. Our feet would scuff through the carpet of brown and yellow leaves as we pounced with cries of triumph on the handsome, mahogany nuts with their birthmark of dullish tan, spilling from their dried-brown husks.

A prize indeed was a pair of "Siamese twins," nuts with identical contours nestled together in the same thick burr.

When the bell rang, we left our hoards all of a heat in the grass beside the old wooden steps of the schoolhouse, piled in wooden strawberry boxes or stuffed in an old sock. The teacher kept a few on her desk to admire, but had no use for them in the classroom.

Briefly, she instructed us on their characteristics — they were called horse chestnuts because the nuts had allegedly once been fed to horses, but they were bitter and inedible to humans. The wood of the tree wasn't worth much either, she said, except for firewood.

Her denigration fell on deaf ears. To us, the horse chestnut tree threw all other trees into the shade.

The pleasures of our childhood were mainly what we were inventive enough to devise from our surroundings. An object of great worth in our eyes could be created from the most mundane materials.

After school, we bored holes in our biggest and best chestnuts and put in a couple feet of string. Twirled in just the right way and let fly, these missiles would shoot up unbelievably high and swift.

Out over the field, just visible against the deep blue sky, they disappeared into the woods. We almost never found them again, but were content to let them lie after that brief moment of glory. Their mission of beauty passed away like a summer cloud.

The smooth, rich patina of the chestnut kindled a special glow in some hidden recess of our hearts, a spark which pulses feebly even now on certain golden October days when the leaves rustle underfoot, the barberries flame up, and the air is scented with the potpourri of autumn.

Haunting Memory

More than the date of Oct. 31 on the calendar, the pungent smell of burning pumpkin takes me back to my first real Halloween, the year I was allowed out on my own.

In a one-room schoolhouse, the upper grades included the fifth through the eighth. My entrance into this elevated status included several new privileges. One of these was "going out" on Halloween.

Our parents didn't become involved in Halloween, so until I was 10 going on 11, the particulars of what was out there on Allhallows Eve were shrouded in mystery.

That afternoon in school, ducking for apples was the highlight of the party. The big tin washtub filled with water was placed in the front of the room, 12 or 15 apples floating on top.

Most of the apples had a coin pressed into them, but it was impossible to tell which they were with our hands clasped (per the rules) behind our backs. Pennies and nickels were fun to find; a silver dime was a real windfall, and one very lucky pupil would find a quarter.

The bigger boys would callously and forcefully push their head right to the bottom of the tub, pushing an apple down and usually getting it the first time. For some of us, this was our initial attempt at the game and getting a merrily bobbing apple in a front-teeth grip took a lot longer.

Afterward, we sat in our seats eating the apples while our hair dried. Refreshments were dark chocolate cupcakes with seven-minute frosting heaped on top, cider and homemade napkin cups filled with candy corn and tiny squirrel nut bars.

After school, I filled an old tin tobacco box with candle stubs and wooden matches. I perfected the air draft on my jack-o'-lantern. The night before I had hollowed it out from one of our best pumpkins, notching the cover just right, cutting the scariest face I could think of.

I also made a window clacker from a wooden spool, a dowel stick and a piece of string. The notched spool was placed against the window glass, held by the dowel and the wound-up string pulled. This made a shattering noise which (hopefully) jolted those inside from their chairs in fright. It wasn't trick or treat in those days — it was just tricks.

My half-black/half-orange jester's costume trimmed with tiny gold bells had been worn by my sisters before me, but I felt transformed as we rode after supper to the church.

Out back by the carriage sheds, as I made my preparations, a nippy wind scurried through the dead leaves, stirring who knew what spooks out of their holes. An almost full moon rode along the tops of the trees, its light turning familiar objects into sinister shapes. Every now and then I glanced up surreptitiously to see if a black witch on a broomstick was outlined against its orange glow. A few bats were making their early evening run from the church steeple, often swooping too close for comfort.

Inside the vestry, my mother was rehearsing for a cantata, The Feast of the Chinese Lanterns, the music making a shield of safety against the unknown. I talked along the green with my jack-o'-lantern lighting the way. I used my clacker on the kitchen window of the parsonage to squeals of fright from within.

Emboldened by success, I ventured farther from the church to a large Victorian house where two maiden ladies lived. Passing their fenced-in pasture, I heard a rustling. I began to talk a little faster. The tiny gold bells sounded too loud in the silence of the unfamiliar night.

Something white moved behind the bushes and my heart thumped in terror. The heat-shrunken cover fell into my pumpkin, putting out the flame. Plunged into darkness, I fled for safety, slowing down only when I saw my mother, a solid, familiar shape, talking with her friends at the church door.

In the security of the front seat of our Ford, I asked my mother to slow down as we passed the pasture on our way home.

"I thought I saw something in there. Do you see anything?" I asked casually.

She peered through the gloom. "Just old Whitey," she said. "Looks like that horse has stayed out late for Halloween," she laughed.

I smiled in the darkness, half-relieved, half-disappointed.

"Yes," I said, with the blase shrug of the seasoned night owl, "I guess all the ghosts and goblins are out tonight."

In Duty Bound

When we got steam heat in the downstairs rooms, my mother joined a bridge club. Warmth was a necessity to be member of "The Jolly Twelve," because meetings were held twice a month in members' homes from November to April

The coal/wood furnace in the cellar was like another presence in the house, breathing away night and day, causing the radiators to steam and clank. Some heat went up the stairs to the bedrooms, but not much to speak of.

The first time I stayed alone in the house was the direct result of the bridge club. November was bad that year, dark and stormy, and I could see my mother was really looking forward to her first afternoon of bridge. That Thursday morning she was full of good spirits and detailed instructions.

"You can have some cookies and milk, then do your practicing," she said. "Fill the wood box, and at 5 o'clock set the potatoes on the front of the stove to boil."

The afternoon was half-spent as I sloshed up the driveway, took down the key from the ledge over the woodshed window, and unlocked the back door.

Sure enough, my mother was gone. Without her always-busy presence, the house seemed to hold its breath. Why was I tiptoeing?

I sat in my father's rocker, feeling like Goldilocks, as I ate a handful of hermits. In the pantry, I ate a lump of brown sugar, debating whether to spring the mouse trap. My mother waged a constant battle, one I considered cruel, with mice. I decided against it.

Going to the woodshed for an armful of wood, I paused to listen to the steady beat of rain on the low roof, a comforting sound. On my second trip, I let the dog in. I could use a little company.

In the parlor, I practiced my piano lesson as the bare branches of the dripping white rose bush scratched against the windowpane. Back in the kitchen, I opened the draft on the stovepipe, put in some wood and pushed the potatoes my mother had left in the kettle full of water, peeled and salted, to the front stove lid. They were soon bubbling away, filling the room with a familiar smell.

Night was closing in as my mother and father arrived home about the same time.

My mother bustled right into the pantry, putting an apron over her best dress. An aura of worldliness hung about her as she recounted her afternoon's experience — the hostess's living room furnished with antiques, the member who actually "smoked, mind you, right in public," and refreshments such as she had never seen.

"Stalks of asparagus, wrapped in little squares of buttered store-bought bread, was one thing," she said.

My father looked up from his newspaper. "Don't sound too filling," he said with his wry smile. "Guess you'd better get on with supper."

My mother paused to look around at the full wood box, the boiling potatoes, the steaming teakettle. Then she looked at me.

"Quite the little lady of the house," she said.

I was glad I hadn't sprung the mousetrap.

The Hurricane

September 1938 was like any other September, the sky blue day after day, the air softly scented with wild grapes. The farm slumbered in end-of-summer somnolence, the growing season past, the harvest well on its way.

As I left for school on Wednesday, Sept. 21, the steamy kitchen already reeked with the smell of spices as my mother put up the last of the pepper relish. On the clothesline, blankets from summer storage were hung for airing. My father and the hired man had left for the Swamp Wood Lot with the heavy wagon and team.

The schoolroom was warm and stuffy. We squirmed in our hard wooden seats, made restless by the hot wind outside the open windows, an oppression in the air.

We had no radio or telephone at school, no contact with the outside world. If our teacher looked worried as she shooed us off the school porch at 3 p.m., it was because of the strange, closed-in smell in the air, a hint of early darkness in the sky.

My mother greeted me at the door. "After you fill the woodbox, I think you ought to run up the hill and tell those folks a hurricane is coming. I heard it on the radio, and the announcer seemed a mite riled up."

Little did my mother know what lay ahead, and for years after chided herself for sending me out on that fateful day.

Glad of the excitement and the importance of delivering such a unique message, I raced down the lane, past the farm pond and up the hill.

Offered buttermilk and cookies, I lingered awhile in the kitchen of the ramshackle house where the elderly Pingrees lived alone.

"It's blowin' some," said old Mrs. Pingree as the sky darkened ominously. "You'd better get on home."

Through the woods, the going wasn't bad, except for a few leaves and twigs coming down. When I reached the field, the full force of the wind hit me, knocking me backward. Bent forward, I skirted the choppy pond, narrowly missed by the branch of an old maple which churned in violent paroxysms of wind and rain.

Thoroughly frightened, my rain-soaked dress plastered to my body, I clung to a telephone pole. As I decided to huddle down under the bank by the side of our lane, I heard my mother's voice above the turmoil, urging me to hurry. I struggled the rest of the way.

Sheltered by the sturdy, familiar walls of the old farmhouse, the real danger I had experienced struck me. Ever since, I have appreciated the meaning of "safe at home."

It wasn't long before the electric power went out. My mother lit the oil lamps and we ate supper.

Outside the windows the trees roared and tossed like mortally wounded beasts before crashing to the ground. The wind shrieked unceasingly, a gigantic force steadily pushing against the walls of the house. Panes of glass blew in and shattered, bricks fell from the chimney, thudding on the shingles.

The huge elm out front was rocked back and forth in the fury of that dark, savage wildness, finally crashing down, almost majestically, on the house roof.

My mother gave up trying to sop up the water coming in, and we sat huddled together on the old studio couch against an inside wall. Objects kept banging against the outside of the house, but by now it was too dark to see.

I slept on the couch that night and woke to a changed, unfamiliar world.

In addition to the huge elm which lay across the lawn resting on the roof, all the old apple trees on the hill were gone. The henhouse was reduced to kindling, and dead hens lay with matted feathers in puddles of rain-soaked leaves. A sheep lay drowned in the brook, which had flooded its banks, washing out the graveled lane.

Late that day my father came home. With bucksaw and ax they had sawed and chopped their way through, with the help of the horses and others along the way. My father and the hired man had spent the night in the woodcutter's shack, deep in the forest, and were unharmed.

The hurricane changed the face of our lives and the landscape of New England.

During the days to follow, we learned how lucky we had been. The hurricane, which came upon us with such scant warning, had claimed 680 lives, destroyed 4,500 buildings, damaged 15,000 structures and smashed 26,000 automobiles.

The winds which blew at more than 100 miles per hour for periods of five minutes at a time and gusted to 130 miles per hour, had demolished familiar and beloved landmarks, crippled the railroads, wiped out electric and telephone service and destroyed most of the apple crop. Entire bridges were swept away, and on the coast the waves towered as high as the buildings.

Tides rose 18 to 25 feet above normal, toppling entire beach settlements, drowning the inhabitants.

No one could have imagined the storm's ferocity, which swept unpredictably from Cape Hatteras northward, building rather than losing momentum, traveling 600 miles in just 12 hours.

I played in the top of a tree that had once seemed to brush the sky and now lay, leaves bruised, wilted and dying, its grandeur cast to the winds. It was hard to make the ravaged world seem believable. Unconsciously trying to bring the incredible disaster to a personal level, I mourned for two girls about my age killed in a school in Massachusetts when a huge chimney fell through the roof.

Nothing was ever quite the same again, our complacency in the natural order of living was shattered. We had been bludgeoned by a savage, unquenchable force, and part of my childhood had been torn away.

A Day to Remember

We knew it as Armistice Day, the anniversary of the signing of the Armistice on Nov. 11, 1918, ending a four-year world war. The great war had touched my life directly in only two ways.

One was a book in the library, a collection of black-and-white photos taken on various battlefields of Europe. The graphic and grisly illustrations were forbidden material for young people, but unlike my mother, the elderly librarian didn't have eyes in the back of her head. So it wasn't difficult to steal a horrified look at the torn and mutilated bodies; my first look at human death.

The second grim reminder was an uncle who had a silver plate in the roof of his mouth. His palate was gone due to an injury sustained on some battlefield; the guttural sounds he made only faintly resembled the English language. Too, he had been shell-shocked and often began to shake for no discernible reason.

In the schoolroom, Miss Crosby read the long, official Armistice Day proclamation, which contained such inspirational phrases as "filled with solemn pride"; "heroism for their country's service," and "gratitude for victory."

Our teacher passed around a picture of the Tomb of the Unknown Soldier, and told us about the most important Armistice Day celebration of all, when the casket of one unidentified American soldier was lowered into that tomb, symbolizing all the unknown dead.

Skinny, who excelled in geography, was sent to the big pull-down map of France to point out the scenes of the major battles, places like Belleau Wood and Chateau Thierry. Sixteen years later, Skinny was killed in another part of France in a different war.

Maurice, who detested "getting up front," read the last verse of *I Have a Rendezvous with Death*, which our teacher said was one of the greatest poems of the World War.

"And I to my pledged word am true,
I shall not fail that rendezvous," he recited, ending with a sigh of relief that his ordeal was over. He, too, kept his rendezvous many years later.

After I read *In Flanders Fields*, Miss Crosby said we could sing some patriotic songs. When Maurice suggested "How're you gonna keep 'em down on the farm, after they've seen Paree," we all laughed until Old Crosseyes rapped her desk with a ruler.

She chose two Civil War songs "Tenting Tonight" and "The Battle Cry of Freedom." Though they were from a different war, she said they now took on a new and deeper meaning.

At 11 a.m., the hour when the guns had become silent along the Western front, we observed two minutes of silence to honor the dead.

We sat with folded hands, in somber stillness, awed by the impressive words we had heard, the vivid imagery, the spectre of war in our midst.

A piece of wood settled with a dull thud inside the wood stove, a last lingering leaf drifted down outside the windows. In our simple, childlike way, we remembered the host of soldiers and sailors who had made our village, our country "safe for democracy."

We could not know that Armistice Day as we knew it would fail to fulfill its promise as the end of all war, that in our entire lifetime the search for peace would be fruitless.

Washday Memories

When school began in the fall, I missed some of the chores round the house, jobs I thought I disliked, but seemed rewarding in retrospect.

Like washdays, which were, of course, on Monday. My first memory is standing on a stool at one of the set tubs, stirring the clothes in the bluing water with a wooden paddle while my mother scrubbed away on the soapy washboard in the other tub.

With electricity came the big, round Easy washer. Mounted on small rubber wheels, it was pushed into position at the set tubs each week and plugged in the overhead light socket. Its agitator action washed the clothes faster and cleaner, and they could be left swishing away as long as desired.

After washing, the clothes were run into the rinse water through the attached electric wringer, a device which won hands-down over the arduous, wrist-wrenching hand-wringing, but which was not selective in what it wrung out.

Once an article was grasped in its smooth rubber rollers, there was no turning back except by pushing a lever on the side. If it was the fingers of your right hand that were caught, it was hard to reach the lever with your left hand to reverse the action.

If a member was missing from church or the ladies society, the explanation might be: "She run her arm up the wringer."

The huge pile of crumpled clothes on the sink-room floor would slowly diminish — the white loads first, the colored clothes, the heavy work clothes, and finally the rugs — washed, spun through the jaws of the wringer into the set tubs to rinse, back through the wringer and into the big wicker basket.

The clothes were always hung in the precise same order, from sheets to socks, to suits of long underwear. All had their appointed place, and if you were sent to the clothesline to get a clean dishtowel on washday, you always knew just where it would be.

The clothes yard was a little distance from the back door to get away from the shade of the elms. I would carry the bag of round, wooden clothespins and keep them accessible as my mother moved along the lines.

Every woman tried to have her laundry flapping in the breeze as early as possible in the morning, and some women had made a much-respected reputation for "getting her clothes on the line at sunup." Leaving the clothes out overnight was unthinkable; forgetting them until they were "night-damp" was almost as bad.

The washer was drained by the pailful, covered with its big, round aluminum lid, and pushed back into a corner of the pantry until next washday. The heavy wooden cover was put back over the set tubs, making it into counter space.

By the time we sat down to a supper that usually featured hash made with Sunday's leftover roast, the kitchen, pantry and sink room were all back in order, the laundry folded and put away or stored in the ironing basket. All that remained was a clean, soapy smell.

Drawing In

The period of growth was ended. The fields and woods stretched bare and dreary, the blaze of autumn glory past. Mornings, the dead leaves lay frost-soaked under the sun's waning warmth, a chill rising from the earth.

The line storm had come and gone, with raging wind and three days of steady downpour. The landscape, drab and stripped, was brightened here and there by the red of drooping barberry, the maroon of sumac seed clusters, the belated green of brittle deep grass along the fence. Gone were the delicate pinks, blues and pale yellows of summer. These were the strong, deep colors of late autumn.

November is a quiet month, nature brooding in a gaunt stillness, waiting for a long winter's sleep.

The rhythm of our lives changed as well. My father, reprieved from the wood lots and far-flung fields, was likely to be somewhere around the place, repairing stone walls, mending harness or sorting apples in the third cellar. At night he often sat late by the kitchen stove, secure in the knowledge of summer days well-spent, his year's work fulfilled.

In the cool darkness of the cellar beneath him were shelves laden with jars of preserves — fruits, vegetables and jellies. On the stone floor sat crocks of pickles and eggs in water-glass. The vegetable bin was full to bursting with big, rough-skinned blue Hubbard squash, baskets of potatoes, carrots packed in sand.

My mother had finished her fall cleaning. All the doorsills had a new coat of paint, the china closet had been turned out, the quilts and blankets aired on the clothesline. Geranium slips struggled for life in the south windows, their glass sparkling from a scouring with vinegar and water.

The parlor had been closed off for the winter, and the door to the front hall was kept shut. The kitchen and sitting room, where we would spend our waking hours for the next six or seven months, were heated by the big kitchen stove.

After school, I sat at the oilcloth-covered kitchen table doing my homework. On the shelf, the wooden mantel clock ticked loudly. Over my head on the wooden accordian rack, dishtowels hung to dry, and on the back of the stove the teakettle bubbled softly.

94

I could smell the potatoes baking in the oven; salt cod was soaking in an iron pan. This meant creamed salt fish for supper, a cold weather meal we hadn't tasted since last spring. The kitchen rocker was decked out in new cretonne cushions; on the newly scrubbed rag rug, the yellow cat was a soft heap of comfort.

Taking my jacket from a hook behind the door, I went to shut up the hens. The dog hung about the steps, waiting for his chance to slink in behind the stove.

It had been a chill, gray day, but a slit of sunset had broken through a rift in the clouds, a streak of brilliant burnt orange, like a banner raised in farewell to autumn.

I climbed up on the shed roof to watch those final rays touch the top of the oak-crowned hill. From there, I would be able to hear the kitchen door slam as my father came in to supper, just about the time the first star appeared in the blackening sky.

The Cellar

Cellars went out of fashion quite some time ago. In the newer houses we have "basements" and "lower levels." With their recreation rooms, laundry rooms, hobby corners and even bedrooms, these below-ground quarters bear scarce resemblance to the cellar of long ago, with its cobwebbed rafters, dirt-stained cement floor and damp stone walls.

Our cellar was vast, divided into three chambers. It was hard to conceive the amount of labor expended in digging this cavernous hole by the shovelful, of dragging in the rocks on a stone boat for the foundation and walls, of heaving them into place.

The first area was the most habitable; it had a window and the wooden bulkhead opened up into the blue sky above. Here were the laden preserve shelves and food storage cabinets. To one side was my father's workbench, a maze of homemade drawers and compartments filled with bits of harness, nuts, bolts, pieces of chain and innumerable odds and ends of accumulated hardware for which a use might one day be found.

In a nook at the brick base of the old kitchen fireplace, where some warmth seeped down from the chimney, was Buster's winter bed, a nest of burlap sacks.

"Put the dog down cellar," my mother would say each night as I prepared for the long trip through the creaking, unheated hallways to my cold bedroom.

Reluctantly, Buster would leave the warm linoleum behind the kitchen stove where he slept with his nose on my father's felt slippers, cast me a reproachful glance, and slink down the dark stairs.

It was the cellar that made us self-sufficient. Snowed in for a week, we could still live fairly high on the hog, with the provisions stored away in these man-made underground bastions.

Nearly every afternoon I would be sent down cellar for a jar of home-canned vegetables or fruit for supper.

The well-worn wooden risers on the stairs had no backs — behind them was cavernous blackness. Near the bottom, with each step I anticipated a hand or claw reaching out to grasp my ankle.

The top half of the cellar way supported shelves on all sides lined with cans, bottles and boxes of medicines and remedies; mixtures such as boric acid, Epsom salts, Argyrol, ground flaxseed, Creolin and stove polish.

There were no mice in the cellar; they preferred the attic

where they made nests of feathers and down pillaged from the blanket chests, raiding the pantry through a maze of nooks and crannies known only to themselves.

The second cellar was closed off by a rough wooden partition and door. An ingenious lighting arrangement had been made; a string on the outside ran through a hole in the wall to the chain on the single light bulb inside. It saved groping around in the dank semidarkness beyond the door.

As a child, I was seldom sent to this isolated vegetable vault; it was the adult's province. Accompanying my mother to this tomblike room, I would watch as with a sharp hatchet she severed a huge Blue Hubbard squash into totable pieces; dug limp carrots from a bin of sand; filled a small basket with dusty potatoes; or dipped out a chunk of salt pork.

Carefully, she would shut the door, pull out the light and we would struggle up the stairs with our swag, emerging into the warm, bright kitchen, which was, surprisingly, just as we left it. To a child, the trip to that far-flung chasm seemed a long and perilous journey.

Farthest back under the house was the apple cellar, reached by a stone passage, forbidding as a castle dungeon.

Here, there was no electricity; work was done by flickering lantern light. In one corner was an old well, caved in, but its 2- or 3-foot depth still filled with crystal-clear water. There were no windows to dispel the gloom; a rotting staircase led up to an unused, heavy trapdoor.

In autumn, the apple cellar was piled to the rafters with bushels of fruit; by spring all this produce would have been sold at market, that cellar empty.

On winter nights, sitting around the kitchen table as snow sifted against the windows, my mother would lift the stove cover often to replenish the wood. When red sparks clung and crackled on the soot-blackened bottom of the cover she would say, "Colder weather ahead."

My older sister would be sent to the cellar for a bottle of cider. Heated in a pan on the stove, with a piece of rolled cinnamon and a few cloves thrown in, it made a drink to warm your heart, fit for the Gods of Olympus.

We drained our big white cups, took a last molasses cookie before my mother carried the jar into the pantry.

"Put the dog down cellar," my mother said. We heard his paws shuffling as he descended to sleep deep in the heart of our stronghold amid the largess of a summer's labor safely stored away; while two floors above, well-provided and secure, we peacefully slumbered.

Under the Weather

Only once during my childhood did I "have the doctor."

In the summer of my fifth year, with first grade looming on the horizon, the white-haired doctor from a neighboring larger town stopped by on his rounds one day to give me a vaccination.

I sat in the old velour-covered Morris chair in the sitting room rigid with trepidation, while my mother, supposedly holding my hand but actually pinning me in place, averted her eyes as the needle went home in my upper arm.

Back then, the phrase "I don't feel good" elicited an instant response, a cool, work-roughened hand on my forehead, a look at my tongue. Dread diseases stalked our lives — polio, scarlet fever, diphtheria, measles.

I would be installed on what I called "the sick couch," in the warm sitting room where my mother could keep an eye on me. Pillows and blankets were brought down from the chilly bedroom. I could hear all the comforting sounds from the kitchen — the clink of china, the rattle of stove lids, the rhythmic beating of the wooden spoon in the big yellow bowl.

At regular intervals, doses of nitre were administered to bring the fever down. At noon, I could count on a mealy baked potato mashed up with milk; for supper it was always creamed toast with a spoonful of grape jelly on the side.

Those days, I got to listen to my mother's favorite radio programs, *Helen Trent* and *Ma Perkins*, although the combination of their hushed dialogue and the nitre usually put me off to sleep.

If there was no fever, treatment was less extensive but far more stringent. A sore throat was perhaps the worst.

My mother's experienced eye could detect the least difficulty in swallowing.

"Does your throat hurt?" she would ask.

"Only a little, I don't need anything," I would say, pushing my breakfast aside and preparing to escape.

Over by the window she would peer down my throat. Finding it red, she would go outside to the lilac bush and break off a good-sized twig. On the end she twirled a small piece of cotton. Dipping this in the Argyrol bottle, she proceeded to paint my throat with the viscous, brown, evil-smelling antiseptic until I gagged. I was then sent off to school.

For internal disorders, there was Nujol, and for cuts and scrapes, a soaking in creolin and water or a dab of iodine. Splinters were removed with a needle sterilized by holding it over a burning wooden match.

One summer in my barefoot days, I cut the bottom of my foot quite badly on a piece of rusty metal. In a day or two, it had festered, and my mother strapped a strip of salt pork firmly in place.

I can still remember the squishy, moist feeling as I limped around. When she took it off, the skin was pure white and wrinkled but the wound was clean as a whistle.

A cold meant a big glob of Vicks rubbed over your chest at bedtime, covered with a piece of flannel, or worse yet, a "steam," your face held over a bowl of hot water with a towel draped over your head.

Sick days were few and far between, but the extra care and cosseting make them stand out in memory. I can hear the sound of the creaking cellar stairs as my mother went down to bring up a jar of homemade root beer.

As I slowly sipped this special treat, watching the bubbles rise, I knew my mother had been worried because I was really sick, and now we both knew I was getting well.

Snow in the Air

As faltering flakes of snow dropped a silvery veil over the meadows and woodlands, we were shut in a deep, white silence. The first big snowfall meant different things to each of us.

To my aged, widowed grandmother it meant another winter to live through, her rheumatic knees and fingers brittle and twisted like the gnarled black branches on the bare trees.

To our teacher, it meant puddles of melted snow-water under the desks, the smell of mittens steaming on the stovepipe, and the opportunity to read aloud John Greenleaf Whittier's *Snow Bound.*

My mother would get out our long, brown cotton stockings, the union suits and black buckle overshoes.

To the children, it meant a number of things, depending on the type of snow, all of them pleasurable.

If the first fall was light and fluffy, we would be allowed to scoop up a bowlful, mix it with vanilla or cocoa and sugar, and enjoy snow ice cream. Along the edge of the woods, rabbit tracks would appear, fun to follow through the quiet, white forest. Only rarely would we see the small brown-tailed animals.

Now and then a blue jay would scream in protest at our presence, or a dusting of snow would sift down from an overburdened hemlock branch. A light snow was useless for sledding, but was easy to clean off the pond for skating.

A heavy, wet snow brought out the sleds and toboggans. Big snowballs were rolled to make snowmen. Snow forts were carefully sculpted with hidden underground caches of snowballs in case the fortress was stormed by the enemy, holed up in a similar stronghold a throwing distance away.

The most gratifying kind was the snow that began in the late evening, all night busily piling up and drifting in every nook and corner as we slept. We would awaken to a world transformed, every bough, fence pole and even the tattered weed stalks ridged with a mantle of white. The only sound in the vast, muffled landscape was the chirp of the chickadee as it flitted from bush to tree.

At dawn, the gray smoke rose lazily from the kitchen chimney as our world slowly came to life. The scrape of the shovel breaking a path to the barn brought a chorus of querulous sounds from the horse stalls and sheep pens.

As the wind beat snow against the icicled windows, when nothing stirred under a blanket of white, the berry bowl was like a tiny piece of the forest floor magically surviving along with us, adding a splash of nature's color to the often dreary, midwinter days.

One night I sat at the round oak table in the sitting room, struggling with my homework.

The temperature had been below zero for three days. Our teacher had told us of starving people standing in bread lines; of families losing their homes through foreclosure now living in cardboard shacks; of despairing farmers out west burning their crops. The Lindbergh's baby boy had been kidnapped; the ship *Morro Castle* had burned with my father's second cousin aboard. Then too, our supper would be boiled carrots and potatoes for the fourth time this week.

But still, Roosevelt said prosperity was "just around the corner"; up in Canada five girl babies, quintuplets, had been born; Babe Ruth had hit his 700th home run; the bread pudding for dessert, though minus raisins, would be sweet and custardy. And in her seemingly bottomless button box, my mother had unearthed enough navy blue buttons to make my jacket, with the sleeves let down, look like new.

On the sideboard, decked out in a bright-red ribbon sat the berry bowl, the adder's-tongue standing tall and straight, pushing strongly against the glass cover.

WINTER

November Nights

November came, with chilly gray days, one after the other. The big, square bedrooms grew slowly colder as the brilliance of autumn was washed away in the cold rains. They were no longer a place to spend time.

The big, black stove became the center of the house. We could bring our clothes and dress in front of the open oven door. It cooked the food, warmed the kitchen and sitting room, burned refuse and heated water. Dishtowels dried on a rack overhead, and before long, mittens would be steaming dry on the stovepipe.

Like the stripped, hushed landscape, we waited for the fall of the first snow. The harvest was over, the fields empty (except for the parsnips which were left in the ground to sweeten until early spring), the cellars full. My father had caught just the right winnowing wind for the cranberries, blowing almost a bushel free of chaff and leaves before storing them away.

As I came in from school, my mother would often say, "Your father wants you in the apple cellar after you've changed your clothes."

The apple cellar, a dim, goose-skin-cold recess far under the big farmhouse, was reached by a stone passageway. Here a let-down bench had been ingeniously installed for sorting apples, with legs on hinges to fold up out of the way when not in use. The flickering kerosene lantern gave off the smell of heat, but no warmth.

Here the handsome Red Astrachans (my mother's favorite), the Baldwins, the hardy Gravensteins and popular MacIntosh were all packed to perfection in wooden boxes, ready for market. Somehow, my father always knew if one of the crisp, red beauties was missing from the top of a box, but we seldom took one anyway. It spoiled the satisfaction of savoring the apple he offered in his own way, keeping us always Argus-eyed, if we had worked hard at the packing.

"If you catch it, you can have it," he would say, tossing one of the biggest and best in our direction. We seldom missed; that meant a dirty and bruised apple as our only reward for an hour or two of work.

One late November day I found a big, fuzzy caterpillar clinging to the edge of a box. His thick coat surely meant a frigid winter to come. Scooping it up on a piece of shingle, I carefully carried it up the bulkhead stairs, where a miserable slit of purple sunset shone in the west. I placed the caterpillar under the frost-crisped leaves to find its own way.

Washing up at the kitchen sink, I could smell the peculiar, rich, spicy aroma of tiny Seckel pears stewing. My mother was frying sweet potatoes at the stove, the sizzling grease hissing as she cut each orange slice into the black iron pan. The cat, Greymalkin, rubbed against her ankles, coming back no matter how many times she impatiently pushed him away with her foot.

The fire crackled cheerfully, my father settled into the old rocker in the corner by the window to read the paper before supper. My mother shook out a clean tablecloth and I set the table, carefully placing the familiar dishes and silverware, the big, white china cups, the cut-glass vinegar cruet and covered butter dish. It was dark outside the heat-steamed windows as the old mahogany clock on the kitchen shelf struck 6 and my mother took a pan of crusty biscuits from the oven.

I thought of the caterpillar, alone in the nest of leaves, hoping it might still be able to spin itself a warm cocoon for shelter in the long wintery days ahead.

The Adder's Tongue

My mother made berry bowls. Today I suppose these glass containers filled with tiny plants would be called terrariums; back then there was no such fancy name.

Early in November, the small round glass bowls with fitted covers were taken from the china closet shelves, washed and polished.

The partridgeberries, gathered before the first snow covered them from sight, spread over the ground in profusion all through the forests. The small, paired variegated evergreen leaves on the creeping stem were pretty in themselves; the one or two scarlet berries on each frond added the crowning touch.

Foraging the plants for the berry bowls was a highlight of late autumn. My mother and her friend made an afternoon of it, ranging far afield, walking perhaps miles. Their chatter and laughter stirred echoes in the chill depths of the November woods as they searched under the fallen leaves with stiff, cold, earth-stained fingers, filling their baskets with sheaves of partridgeberries, clumps of various mosses.

Each year, my mother made a special search for the elusive adder's-tongue, an unfernlike fern that for her represented the ultimate attainment. The adder's-tongue, around which a lot of folklore had gathered, imbuing the plant with magical properties, held a special symbolism for her, like a talisman. The plant, a single green leaf with a netted pattern, handsome in its simplicity, grew sparsely in moist meadows, damp thickets.

It was a good omen when my mother found a patch. She uprooted only a single plant to preserve the rare species.

"Did you find one?" I asked, as she covered her basket with a wet burlap bag to keep the plants fresh.

She nodded and smiled in a special way, like the greatest gift of the gods had been laid at her feet.

The berry bowls were assembled with dampened moss at the bottom, the tiny partridgeberry vines intricately interwoven around the sides, hairy roots hidden.

By Christmas, the berries would be plumper, the leaves ever so lush and shiny, clustered against the sparkling glass.

Besides our own, there was a bowl for the ladies society Christmas fair; one for my Boston aunt; one for my married sister.

As the wind beat snow against the icicled windows, when nothing stirred under a blanket of white, the berry bowl was like a tiny piece of the forest floor magically surviving along with us, adding a splash of nature's color to the often dreary, midwinter days.

One night I sat at the round oak table in the sitting room, struggling with my homework.

The temperature had been below zero for three days. Our teacher had told us of starving people standing in bread lines; of families losing their homes through foreclosure now living in cardboard shacks; of despairing farmers out west burning their crops. The Lindbergh's baby boy had been kidnapped; the ship *Morro Castle* had burned with my father's second cousin aboard. Then too, our supper would be boiled carrots and potatoes for the fourth time this week.

But still, Roosevelt said prosperity was "just around the corner"; up in Canada five girl babies, quintuplets, had been born; Babe Ruth had hit his 700th home run; the bread pudding for dessert, though minus raisins, would be sweet and custardy. And in her seemingly bottomless button box, my mother had unearthed enough navy blue buttons to make my jacket, with the sleeves let down, look like new.

On the sideboard, decked out in a bright-red ribbon sat the berry bowl, the adder's-tongue standing tall and straight, pushing strongly against the glass cover.

The Kitchen Stove

The big black stove in the huge kitchen was the heart of the house. In winter, the dining room did double duty as a sitting room, with couch, Morris chair and radio. The stove heated both rooms, as well as a small sink-room off the kitchen. The pantry, meant to be cold, was partitioned off.

A hole with a closable iron grating was cut in the dining room ceiling; some warmth rose into the chamber above, but was quickly disseminated in the chill of the upstairs hall and adjoining roomy chambers.

The kitchen stove looms large in memory as the weather turns frosty, because we were never cold in our daytime living quarters. The stove burned steadily, never failing. If the heat became overpowering, we could always open the door.

The stove and built-in woodbox took up one whole wall, installed where a fireplace had been torn out. The black pipe went straight up, then turned with an elbow piece into the flue. The pipe itself got very hot and was the best place for drying wet mittens and heavy socks. Leather boots, my father's felt slippers and our dog Buster kept warm behind the stove. Weak, scarcely breathing newborn lambs had been warmed into life by the oven; cats curled up on the rug in front.

All around this radiant cast-iron fortress were places to put your feet; one side held a shelf with a little door for cleaning out the ashes, the oven had a protruding ledge and silver "bumpers" were wrapped around just above the legs. On the other side was a rectangular covered reservoir for keeping hot water always on hand. In winter, soapstones and bricks used to warm the beds were heated there.

Even on hot summer days, the fire in the stove was often kept mulling along until bedtime. There was no other way to get a cup of hot tea or brew a pot of coffee should a neighbor drop by.

There were four round stove lids, two right over the firebox where fast cooking took place, two next to these for medium heat and space beyond that for keeping food warm. The capacious black teakettle was always on the back of the stove — a push forward put it on the simmer.

A handle with a wire grip fitted into grooves in each stove lid for lifting; a poker hung on a nail beside the woodbox. A painted tobacco tin filled with wooden matches sat on the shelf beside the clock.

108

My mother ran the stove — she was the keeper of the flame, supremely cognizant of its responses to wind and weather. She controlled the dampers with a master's touch; cleaned out the ashes on schedule to keep the draft clear.

Periodically, she let the fire die down and polished all the outside surfaces, using a big bottle of Black Cat Stove Polish kept in the cellar way, achieving a luster sleek as ebony.

When she came home from church or a meeting of the ladies society, my mother hustled to the stove even before taking off her hat, rattling the lids, poking the coals, putting in wood.

In summer, she knew how to build a "supper fire" — a small, hot fire that quickly did the job and spent itself. On the coldest winter nights, she stoked the smoky maw with chunk wood — an unsplittable piece of tree crotch or bulky oak.

Just after dawn, a stir of the glowing ashes and a few slivers of split pine coaxed the fire into crackling life, sending up from the tall chimney a straight column of gray smoke, a signal that the farm day had begun.

Cooking on the wood stove, keeping the temperature consistent for baking, was an art; so was filling the woodbox. Several types of wood had to be always close at hand; otherwise my mother would be forced into a quick trip to the woodshed.

The hired man did a bang-up job on the woodbox, but when I was old enough to take the job over, things didn't run as smoothly. If I was awakened in my frigid bedroom by the sound of the ax on the chopping block, I knew there were breakers ahead.

"Why you can't remember a simple thing like filling the woodbox I'll never know," my mother would scold as I dressed in front of the now-glowing heat.

Casting down my eyes in repentance, I would sit in my place at the oilcloth-covered table, listening to the cornmeal mush crackle in the black spider; the splutter of frying eggs; the squeak of the loose floorboard as, head bent over the stove, my mother shifted from one foot to the other.

The kitchen smelled of dusty bark and woodchips, drying dishtowels, baking bread, boiling jelly, spattered lard, steamed fruit, singed chicken feathers and popcorn shaken in a wire basket right over the coals.

Coming in from out-of-doors, you were embraced by waves of this aromatic, steamy warmth, laced with tendrils of wood smoke. You were home.

The kitchen was never the same after the shiny white, pristine gas stove was installed. Two ugly silver tanks were set up under the window beside the syringa bush. When you sat in the kitchen rocker, there was no place to prop your feet for comfort on a cold day.

The kettle no longer steamed; the stove was turned on only at cooking time. No pine knots hissed and crackled. The room was silent, diminished.

The garbage and newspapers could not now be burned — they were stored in the shed to be hauled away. The kitchen smelled faintly of gas, of dampness under the sink, of cold linoleum.

Life was easier for my mother. A steam radiator gave out desultory heat, hot water gushed from a gleaming faucet at the sink, the cooking flame was available at the turn of a knob, predictable, adjustable.

But the enveloping warmth, the glow, the bustle of life-sustaining struggle, were missing. The anchor that moored us to childhood was gone.

Making Music

Just about every house in town had a piano, and ours was no exception. Our mahogany veneer upright stood in the front room, along with the walnut glass-fronted bookcase, the uncomfortable grape-carved sofa, the marble-topped candlestand and the Victorian side tables.

Each tabletop was covered with a beautifully ironed, embroidered dresser scarf or doily. The brightly patterned carpet covered most of the floor — around the edges was painted a dark brown.

The front room was actually a parlor, unused most of the time, and unheated. We used part of the dining room as a sitting room, and the front room was kept in pristine condition. My mother dusted with kerosene on a rag, so every surface was shining.

Twice a year, she entertained her bridge club there, turning on the steam radiator the night before to get it warm. For me, the front room was for piano practice. It was another "cultural advantage."

My teacher was considered exclusive because she used all three of her names, never just a middle initial, and had a breakfast nook, a modern innovation. She was plumpish, and blond, and always dressed to the nines. I walked to and from my lesson, a 2-mile trip, carrying my music in an old leather briefcase of my father's.

It soon became apparent I had no talent at the piano. I had an ear for music, but not the technical facility to make a good pianist. My fingers stumbled, faltered and tortured the melody.

Every weekday, I pounded away while the sunlight slanted lower from the window to the west, or the little sparrow sat on a branch of the elm tree, singing in the rain. In the winter, the front room door was left open for extra warmth, but it was still cold.

An hour a day seemed a long time to practice, but as I progressed I began to enjoy the more romantic songs such as "Play Gypsies, Dance Gypsies," and "Some Day My Prince Will Come," and strove to play smoothly.

Fluency never came, much as I longed to be able to sit gazing out the window at the new moon as my fingers moved dreamily over the keys, as shown in the frontispiece of one of Myrtle Reed's books.

It wasn't the teacher's fault — she had many exceptional pupils, one of whom was my friend Miriam. We started lessons together, yet I was still plodding along in *Book I* while she had advanced to the third level of Duvernoy. I know my mother, who could ill-afford the lessons, had visions of me as pianist of the Grange, accompanist for the ladies society, or even a substitute at the church organ.

It wasn't meant to be. After five years, I could play hymns fairly well, and had memorized "Fur Elise" as a stock offering when asked to perform.

Miriam's mother came to tea one June day, and from the front steps, where I was doing my homework, the conversation was clearly audible.

"Miriam has been asked to play in a concert," said our guest.

My mother made suitable, though restrained, remarks, no doubt bracing herself for the next question, which was:

"How's Elinor doing?"

I heard my mother's best china cup clink into her saucer.

"Well," she said, "you can't fit a square peg into a round hole."

I knew then it was all over. I convinced my mother to trade our piano for a player piano, and for years after, the strains of "My Wonderful One," "Let the Rest of the World Go By," and other favorites echoed fluently and unfalteringly through the rooms of the old house.

Thanksgiving Dinner

Thanksgiving Day in memory is always cold and cloudy, the kind of day you could easily picture a wild turkey walking in and out among the stumps of the trees.

Turkey was on my mind then, for when I was growing up we never ate turkey except at Thanksgiving. Turkeys were raised with that single, all-important day in mind, and the anticipation of Thanksgiving dinner rose to great heights.

The dinner was what Thanksgiving was all about in those days. Smoke curled all night from the kitchen chimney as my mother kept the fire up to cook the 20-plus pound turkey.

The night before, she had packed its white, blue-veined body with her own special stuffing — bread broken into small pieces, onion, melted butter, sage and poultry seasoning. Her stuffing was always moist and rich, "the best part of the bird," my father said.

The turkey had to be ready for dinner just after noon, since we always ate at 1 p.m. My father, even on that day, wouldn't "waste the whole afternoon."

Early on, my mother, in her best bib apron, was in the kitchen. Laughing at the tears in her eyes, she was peeling tiny white onions. Traditionally, there would also be mashed potatoes, and creamy squash or fluffy whipped turnip. In a small blue bowl sat a quivering mound of ruby cranberry sauce, made from berries picked before the first hard frost in the meadow. Another once-a-year luxury was the store-bought bunch of celery, cut in finger-sized lengths to fit the cut-glass celery dish.

My job, using a brick and hammer, was to crack the mixed nuts loosely for the nut bowl, so they could easily be picked out of the shell and eaten. Placed nearby the bowl was a set of six silver nut picks and a cracker.

Long after the white morning frost had disappeared from the bare branches of the trees, sounds began to emanate from the dwelling place; the rattle of dishes and silverware, the laughter of cousins and aunts and grandchildren brought together for the holiday.

The smells from the kitchen grew stronger, all the fragrances mingled into a steamy aroma that clamored "Thanksgiving."

My brother-in-law fitted three leaves into the big oak dining table and my sister unfurled the huge, white damask tablecloth like a banner.

The "well-to-do" aunt and uncle from Western Massachusetts arrived in their chic blue four-door sedan, amid a flurry of expensive perfume, pipe tobacco and fur coats (they each had one). They had brought a fruitcake and a glass jar of candy from S.S. Pierce in Boston.

In the early afternoon the feast was at last ready, the voluminous, carefully ironed white napkins and sparkling water goblets in place, along with the compartmented green glass plates.

The laden serving dishes were carried in, and last of all, the huge turkey on the willoware platter.

We took our seats in front of the place cards painstakingly fashioned from spruce cones by my sister and me.

As we sat down, my mother looked hot and tired, but well-satisfied with her efforts. She had found time to take off her apron, smooth her hair and pin on her cameo brooch.

On the pantry shelves waited pumpkin and mince pies, and the steamed plum pudding kept warm on the back of the stove, the rum sauce ready to serve in a pitcher nearby.

After dinner, the fruit and nut bowls would be carried into the rather chilly parlor, opened up for the day. There, most of us would sing around the piano, always ending with my favorite, "The Landing of the Pilgrim Fathers."

This inspirational song of courage, like the turkey platter, was resurrected only once a year, but the words echo in memory still:

The heavy night hung dark,
The hills and waters o'er;
When a band of exiles moored their bark
On the wild New England shore."

The Blizzard

The kitchen was dim; the one oil lamp ineffectual against the sullen clouds, a leaden sky. The frozen world, already covered with several inches of snow accumulated inch by fluffy inch since the January thaw, was hushed, waiting.

With his finger, my father melted a hole in the frost-foliaged windowpane to scan the outdoor thermometer for a second time.

"Dropping," he said. "A cold front's coming down from up north. Likely heavy snow," he predicted, after a look at the weather vane on the barn roof.

My mother wrapped an extra scarf around my throat against the chill, damp bitterness and sent me off.

In the schoolyard, the flag had not been raised. A fine, powdery snow had started, slowly sifting down in the pure, keen air. These flakes were not big, wet "goose feathers." This snowstorm meant business, obscuring the somber gray hills, presaging more to come.

As we stood to salute the flag, little eddies of white were whirling off the eaves, swirled by a keening wind. A small flock of snowbirds flew by, heading for shelter.

We bent to our lessons, the storm momentarily forgotten. Snow was a familiar phenomenon in our lives, an act of nature beyond our control. Schoolwork was our immediate concern.

Miss Crosby guided us through arithmetic, unable to keep her eyes from straying to the window every few minutes; unable to find the heart to chide us for doing the same.

The wind, playfully whispering at first, had picked up; the snowfall steadily increased in density; tiny white drifts piled the windowpanes.

By lunchtime, wind-driven snow was whirling over the fields, totally surrounding our isolated building, attacking from every side. There was no question of going out for noon recess. After we put our lunchboxes away, old Crosseyes let us play "hangman" on the blackboard as the room darkened ominously.

At 2 o'clock Miss Crosby, her face sort of pinched-looking, interrupted our silent reading. She was a city girl, but had boarded in the country a number of years. She knew a blizzard when she saw one.

"I would like to dismiss you early, but it has gone too far for that," she said, adding that someone would undoubtedly come for us before long.

115

Our feelings hovering between fright and excitement, we waited, listening. Soon we heard the sound of a team. A member of the school committee had brought his wagon-sled to get us all safely home.

Subdued by our teacher's ill-concealed concern as well as by the stern gravity of Mr. Lovett and the unfamiliar situation, we hurriedly put on our outside clothes. Miss Crosby dampered down the stove and pulled the green window shades.

The storm hit us with full force as we ran from the schoolhouse door to the logging sled, piling into the hay-filled wagon bed. Those who lived close to the school would trot closely along behind. Miss Crosby sat up front with the driver as we rode out onto the gale-swept road and set off to the east.

The scudding snow veiled the houses, each with a lighted window, as one by one the children and Miss Crosby were let off at their dooryards. Mr. Lovett, who lived just this side of the village, circled the town, heading into the teeth of the storm first, coming up on my house the back way. I would be the last to get off.

The horses plodded stolidly beneath the laboring tree boughs, through the deepening snow and mounting drifts. The wind shrieked around us, snatching my breath, angrily pelting us with gusts of stinging snow, whitening Mr. Lovett's eyebrows and clinging to the side whiskers below his plaid wool cap.

There was no respite from the assault of the icy, whitened air. We were isolated in Emerson's "tumultuous privacy of storm."

In the old cemetery, dimly perceived gravestones stood like dwarfed, sheeted ghosts. The horses knew the road; their snorting puffs of breath were comforting in that vast, howling wilderness of white.

I remembered the story my mother told each winter, of the little boy in her class who had died years ago on his way home from school in just such a blizzard. He wasn't found for days, having strayed off the snow-obscured road into a field. I moved a little closer to the sturdy bulk of the silent, snow-plastered man by my side, his mittened hands half-frozen to the ice-coated reins. Inside my overshoes, I wiggled my toes, which had lost all feeling.

Chilled and half-hypnotized by the blinding, unrelenting whiteness, I heard Mr. Lovett's muffled voice.

"Here we are," he said, and swung me down into the snow.

Indistinctly, through the white whirlwind, I saw my father struggling down our lane to meet me. I felt a loss as the horses strained forward with new vigor; their barn was not far away.

The kitchen was warm and seemed to glow. My mother fussed around, brushing the snow from my clothes as she hung them to dry; making me a cup of cambric tea; speculating on the ferocity of the storm.

As I lay in bed that night, the wind buffeted the house like the breath of a giant dragon, blowing snow through every crack, smattering the window panes, shaking the timbers in its frigid grasp.

Thinking again of the little boy lost forever in the snow, I snuggled deeper into the secure warmth, grateful for the hot brick at my feet, the sturdy roof, the stout walls. I pulled the quilts up around my ears, shutting out the clamor as the blizzard raged on through the night.

Survivors

My mother's reaction to the end of the blizzard was a flurry of activity. Never would she admit to weakness, but I could sense and my father must have known her fear of being snowed in, trapped and helpless.

Years before, her brother had almost bled to death during a storm; loved ones could be lost forever in the whirling, blinding white fury; children's fevers rose with the winds that shrieked outside the viewless windows.

Softly humming a hymn, she cooked up a platter of fried cornmeal mush, side bacon and thick slabs of homemade bread. She sent me to the cellar for a jar of the best strawberry jam; treated Buster to a dollop of cooking grease in his meal of stale bread and skim milk; and set my father's boots to warm by the hearth.

After breakfast, I trailed behind my father and the hired man as they shoveled a path to the barn and outbuildings. It was slow going; the wind had shaped some drifts almost as high as my head. Branches had fallen from the elms; even pieces of tree bark were strewn about like broken artifacts. Tall weeds along the fence wore tiaras of white.

When we got close, I could hear the sounds of the prisoned animals; the baaing of thirsty sheep; the neigh of hungry horses.

My father rolled back the heavy door, releasing a steamy, fetid odor that told of life within. Fanny, the mare, thrust her long nose over the stall, seeming to indicate with toss of head the empty manger.

The heavy ewes in the lambing pens milled about, gazing at us with large, liquid eyes.

Opening the trapdoor to the cote below, I tossed down an icy snowball, causing the ram to stamp his foot in reproach.

In the loft, a mouse scurried away from the droppings near the covered wooden grain bin. I took a handful of oats, and jumping and rolling through the snow, made my way to the corner of the barn, scattering the seeds for the birds, the mice; whatever wild creature might pass by.

Tiny field mice trails crisscrossed from the snow-mounded juniper bushes on the hillside behind the barn. Rabbit tracks in unmistakable four-pawed symmetry strengthened my resolve to delve into the sand bin in the cellar for a couple of last summer's carrots.

Falling backward, I made a pair of angel's wings in the snow to mark my existence in the impassive, limitless landscape of white marble.

On the lilac bush by the back door, my mother had hung a stale doughnut from a piece of string; chickadees fluttered around, their tiny breasts fluffed by the wind. Blue jays, a brilliant flash of color against the snow, screamed from the trees behind the henhouse; hot mash for the fowls was yet to come.

Late in the afternoon, a sleigh drove in. It was the storekeeper from the village, Mr. Biggs, making a few of his regular deliveries. Sitting at the kitchen table, stirring sugar into a mug of hot tea, he told us the news.

Most of the roads were cleared, he said, except Lily Pond Road, where the wind blowing across the lake made the drifts insurmountable. Tomorrow, he said, a road crew would shovel along with the Monarch snowplow and break through.

Old Mrs. Ellis had hung a red rag as a distress signal out her upstairs window. The men on the plow found her huddled in a rocker, a cat in her lap, the fire out, well on the way to starving and freezing. There was plenty of firewood right in the adjoining woodshed; a pantry full of food.

"She set there a couple days 'fore the plow come," marveled Mr. Biggs. "Storms get to people, somehow," he said. "She just couldn't go it alone."

My mother shivered slightly and set her jaw, refilling our cups with steaming, fragrant liquid.

"Viola was took real bad," continued our messenger, helping himself to another filled cookie. "Tryin' to shovel out them precious hens of hers, her heart must have give out. Will Gordon and his son found her when they was delivering milk, lucky thing, she could have froze solid, lying there. She was breathing, just. They put her on a plank and carried her in the house. Will's gone to the 'Port to fetch the doctor, if the roads is open."

Encouraged by our rapt attention, he shook his head in wonder.

"Strange what a storm can do," he said.

The mail truck from the city that dropped off our incoming mailbag and picked up the outgoing post had got stuck just past the town line the day of the storm, said Biggs. In the winter, the mailman carried with him in the van a pair of snowshoes so he was able to walk back and hitch a ride into the city on a municipal plow.

"He made it through today," said Biggs, "but one of his tire chains ripped a hole in the mudguard coming up Two-Mile Hill."

"Now," he said, "I'd best be on my way before them groceries in the sleigh turns to icebergs."

He slid smoothly down our lane, the man-made path merging with the meadows of untouched new snow. The late-afternoon sun turned the barn windows to smoky orange. The woods beyond were already in shadow. Far back in their depths was the cedar swamp where I pictured a lone red-headed woodpecker drilling in the branch of a dead tree; a feather-booted owl noiselessly stalking its prey, the white-footed mouse; the winding trails of the deeryard piercing the isolation of the forest aisles.

Animals and humans alike, we had strengthened our defenses, girded our spirits; we had survived the storm. Winter held us still clasped in an icy grasp, but nature rested, restoring herself deep within.

Far away a dog barked to be let in. The first star appeared; night fell like a benevolent blanket, wrapping us in its healing silence.

Winter Nights

Our weekday evenings followed a set pattern. I did my homework at the kitchen table while my mother finished up her chores. Just before 7, she stoked up the stove, pulled off the light, hung her apron on the back of the cupboard door and led the way into the adjoining sitting room.

My father was a town official who spent his evenings in the town hall. He and his fellow civil servants held meetings and transacted ever- increasing municipal business for a few hours each night. My mother said it wasn't necessary to put in so much time, but they obviously liked being there.

The town office was a formidable man's domain — a cigar-smoke-filled room, potbellied stove glowing red, sand-filled spittoon, heavy oak table piled with papers. A huge, black built-in vault embossed with gold letters stood open like the maw of a whale, swallowing the tax dollars and spewing them forth in the town payroll. Here my father spent, for 60 years, what could have been his leisure hours.

We were his "womenfolk," the keepers of the flame, so to speak. My mother would draw the dark green shades, shutting out the darkness beyond the frost-foliaged windows. If her mending was caught up, she would take out her crocheting from the sideboard — an ecru pineapple tablecloth — and snap on the table radio.

For an hour, we would listen to *Romance Isle, Fibber McGee and Molly* or Jack Benny. One night we heard Madame Schumann-Heink in a special concert. My mother, who had earned modest local fame as one of the sweetest altos in the church choir, enjoyed this immensely.

The radio was shut off when the nightly program ended; it was never on unless someone was sitting listening.

I would curl up on the studio couch with a book or lay out a game of solitaire on the round oak table. Silence was all around us, the sounds were few; the occasional creak of old timbers as the cold settled deeper into the iron-hard ground, the scratching of Buster's paws on the linoleum as he dreamed of rabbit runs behind the stove, the whine of wind in the eaves.

Pulling aside the shade, I would rub a hole in the crystalline, icy window pane to stare into the black and silver stillness beyond. All her married life in that old farmhouse, I learned in later years, my mother yearned to be able to see a light, a glow in the lonely, cavernous darkness that meant another person was nearby, another soul awake in that frozen world. But there was no dwelling near enough.

The wood burned brightly in the big, black kitchen stove, keeping the arctic chill at bay, though its brittle icy fingers often wrapped a death grip around the exposed water pipes under the sink.

Its hoary frigid breath crept through tiny niches, invading our very living space, whitening the iron latch on the inside of the kitchen door, frosting the corners of the sills.

On the coldest nights we could hear the thick-ribbed ice crack on the farm pond, a sound hard to describe, like the powerful snap of a giant whip.

The sitting room door was shut; beyond it was the front hall, the parlor, the spare room, and upstairs the four chambers, all unheated and out-of-bounds, except for sleeping, until April.

At bedtime, I took a heated brick from the back of the stove, encasing it in an old gray sock, making a dash for the east chamber and the warmth of flannel sheets and heavy quilts.

Secure and snug, a tiny capsule of vitality in the boundless grandeur of a winter night, I drifted toward sleep.

Outside the windows, the north wind whipped up snow spectres in its race across the fields; the angry sting of sleet pelted against the panes; or the myriad stars glittered whitely in the inky blackness of the sky as the white-crusted roof stored up moonlight in the lustrous, sculptured icicles.

The last sound I heard was the crunching of tires on the hard-packed snow as my father turned down our lane, heading for that one lighted window in the vast white silence of pastures, fields and woodlands.

Christmas on the Way

Preparations for Christmas began in the schoolroom right after Thanksgiving. Our art, manual training and sewing classes became workshops for making Christmas gifts.

In art, the four upper grades were making paperweights from glass caster cups. I was fascinated with the small cans of red and green enamel we used to paint the bottoms, superimposing underneath a picture of our choice cut from an old greeting card or catalog. This gift would be for my father. In my mind's eye I could already see it reposing grandly atop important papers on his big roll-top desk in the sitting room.

Sewing class was not as enjoyable. I spent an hour a week fashioning from layers of cloth a pen wiper for my mother, a needle book for my sister, working under Miss Crosby's strict tutelage.

"Handwork requires patience, neatness and careful attention to detail," she reiterated at the start of each session.

"Hold your work *up*," she would admonish, snatching the small, rumpled squares of linen from my lap as I sat hunched over, bidding me to rip it out and begin again.

I looked enviously at the boys who were in the corner by the woodbox working on sloyd, small knives flashing. They had all the luck. I would get a " D " for sure, especially after she saw the spot of blood where I had pricked my finger on the needle.

These school-made presents were important, though, as they were the only ones I would have to give.

As children, we had never heard of "Christmas shopping". Though our parents made occasional trips to the city, store-bought gifts were few, and most of those we received came from the Sears Roebuck catalog. Along with pajamas, slippers, homemade mittens, hats and scarves, I could expect a toy or game and a book or two. Many of my classmates didn't receive even that, but Christmas, to all of us, was still the best time of the year.

Christmas had to be made through our own efforts as families and members of a community. Only a third of the village homes and farms had electricity, fewer still had radios. If we wanted to hear carols, we had to sing; to listen to a Christmas story, someone had to read aloud; to see a play or pageant, we had to put it on ourselves. The women baked our Christmas treats, and the men cut and dragged home the tree. This was the world as we knew it.

The school day was drawing to a close. The air in the room was stuffy, heavy with the smell of paint, wood shavings and drying overshoes. The first three grades, in sing-song voices, were learning the vowels by rote. Maurice as weekly wood-boy was stoking the fire, making the stovepipe crackle. Skinny rattled the dipper in the water pail as he went for his third drink of the afternoon.

It was two weeks 'til Christmas, and at the end of each school day we sang a carol. Miss Crosby went to the piano, and perhaps feeling she had been a little harsh, let me pick the song. I chose "Good King Wenceslaus," because outside the tall windows the snow lay "deep and crisp and even."

We liked the part that went:

"Brightly shone the moon that night,
Though the frost was cruel,
When a poor man came in sight
Gathering winter fuel."

We all could relate to that. Youngest to oldest, we sang well, and after a final flourish of chords, Miss Crosby swung around on the stool and smiled at us as we stood beside our desks.

"Class dismissed," she said.

As I bundled up and wound the knitted scarf tightly around my neck for the long walk home, I took a last look at the windowsill where our caster cups lay drying. Christmas was on its way, and as surely as the sun rises, I knew it would come.

Next week, one of the men on the town committee would bring a tree to the school. We would make colored paper chains that stretched all across the room to encircle it.

On the last day of school before the holiday vacation, Miss Crosby would give us each a wrapped present. Last year it had been a pencil with a Bible verse inscribed on it; the year before, a soft, gum rubber eraser.

My gift to her was to be a handkerchief with a hand-crocheted edging.

She'll sure know I didn't make the edging, I thought ruefully as I stuffed my sewing projects deep in my desk out of sight and ran out into the softly falling snow.

The Man in the Red Suit

Christmas was one of the few times in the hard-working calendar of the farm year when we could feast on beauty, pomp and splendor. Too, it was a religious rekindling and a time of fellowship.

Even the cavernous church sanctuary seemed warmer, with fir boughs and evergreen banked on the altar, the communion table and the windowsills, candles glowing and the joyful voices of the Christmas choir. Except for a tree, few of our homes were decorated; the church was the focal point. Since a child was what Christmas was all about, we were expected to shine.

We stood for hours in tableaus and plodded our way through pageants, trying to keep a straight face when the wild-eyed real live sheep became restive or one of the Wise Men sneezed. Most of us could quote the nativity passages from the Bible word for word. This story was full of puzzling, unexplained mysteries, but we accepted it as the solemn, awesome, reverent part of Christmas.

Santa Claus was an apple of another tree. He was more personal, the fun side of the festivities. Back then, there weren't dozens of Santas around to tarnish the image of this special personage.

In the few pictures we saw of him, Santa always looked exactly the same. Sometimes he had a pipe in his mouth, a human failing which made him all the more endearing.

Perhaps I was lucky about Santa Claus. My parents never told me he wouldn't come if I was naughty. They never told me he would come either, but this was a foregone conclusion. What little doubt I had only added to the anticipation.

If we had a lean Christmas, it was only natural, I reasoned, that Santa would feel the pinch, too. But he always came through in some way until the time when he faded into a knowing smile and a "let's pretend" attitude.

It was comforting to think there was a kind, thoughtful person far away at the end of the earth who would journey through the cold midnight skies to bring us a present. Santa was in a class with the Sugar Plum Fairy, the Velveteen Rabbit and Winnie the Pooh. He filled a real need in our lives, a need for wonder and fantasy and things that go bump in the night.

We saw him once a year at the Sunday school party, and his voice, clothes and demeanor always passed muster. Each year he seemed plumper, his suit a little tighter, but he was a mortal after all. We never got to sit on his lap and rattle off a list of toys we would like — we accepted what came our way — but Santa was the frosting on the cake just the same.

What could match the excitement of hearing sleigh bells in the winter darkness outside the church vestry windows, or the sound of heavy footsteps as he descended the narrow stairs from the vestibule? We sat in breathless silence, all knotted up inside with excitement and anticipation. Was he really *here*?

Shouting and laughing, he burst his red and white presence upon us carrying a well-stuffed burlap bag. The Sunday school tree was decorated with garlands of popcorn and cranberries along with a few handmade ornaments.

Santa took his place beside it and called out our names individually. We each received a small parcel wrapped in white paper and tied with red string, a small net bag of candy and a large orange, in addition to a friendly pat on the head and sometimes a pertinent comment.

As we grew older we found it hard to believe there was a man in a red suit who lived at the North Pole and manufactured toys, impossible to credit that he flew around the world in a sleigh. But in spirit, we still believed in Santa Claus, because we had faith in magic and miracles and the unquenchable warmth of the human heart at Christmastime.

As the years passed, younger children would ask, "Is there really a Santa Claus?"

With a pensive smile we would answer, "What do *you* think?"

Winter Woods

My father worked with wood in all its forms. He had two distinctive aromas about his person; the spicy scent of the bay rum he used after shaving and the fragrant redolence of freshly cut wood, pine pitch and cedar shavings.

He dealt in stove wood and lumber, logs and fence posts, pine limbs for kindling. Starting out as a farmer, he gravitated more and more toward forest work adding new tracts and wood lots to the already vast holdings of his inheritance. Wood was an ingrained force in his spirit.

During a long lifetime, never did he use anything except a wooden match to light a cigar, lantern or fire. Always in his pocket was a smooth-worn, chased-brass match case with a snap top, filled each morning from the big tin matchbox on the kitchen shelf.

Our first electrical appliance was a 20-inch saw blade installed in an open shed, plugged into a dangling open socket by a frayed electrical cord, screaming its way through a load of 6-foot lengths in record time.

Each winter, two brawny French-Canadian lumberjacks were hired to live in a small cabin, fell trees and cut wood deep in the forest.

On the last Saturday of the month, these two "cutters," all slicked up, appeared at the kitchen door for their pay. That night, hitching a ride into the city, they spent their earnings on urban pleasures, returning, according to my father, "stewed as fresh-boiled owls."

We owned a truck with a wooden body, but horse-pulled logging sleds were used in winter to bring out the loads. It was perilous work, especially in the high woods where the slope was steep.

Then a bridle chain was wrapped around the runners to serve as a brake for the loaded sled, digging into the glass-smooth snow of the woods-road. For extra-heavy loads, a thick rope was rigged from the back of the sled to a stout tree at the top of the slope, the line paid out slowly as the sled went down.

The hired man and my father spent day after day in the woodlands. They took a lunch of bread and cheese, pie and bottles of cold tea, placing it near the slash fire to keep from freezing.

One rare day when my father planned a short trip to check on the "boys," as he called the woodcutters, he let me ride along, undoubtedly to "toughen me up."

127

Sitting on the back of the cumbersome sledge, feet swinging just above the snowy track, I watched the miles slide by behind the heavy runners.

Turning onto the cart path, the forest depths were white and still, rattling bare limbs pencil-etched, thick-boughed pines, firs and hemlocks whispering faintly in the stinging wind. The two horses, like fairy steeds glistening in the swirls of snow falling from the branches overhead, plodded along, heads tossing, nostrils steaming.

A quail piped in the underbrush; I imagined in the thicket a deer, escaped from the hunter's quest, safe for another year of freedom in glades and glens scarce seen by human eye.

We stopped at the cutter's cabin; smoke rose lazily from the stovepipe chimney; a pair of snowshoes was propped by the rough plank door. Woodchips and bark were everywhere; a red squirrel disappeared into the loosely stacked woodpile.

This timberland was called "Wildcat Woods"; the undergrowth was close on all sides, huge tree trunks cast gloomy shadows; beady eyes were surely peering from the brushwood, snow-hushed paws silently stalking.

As shadows lengthened, an icy chill crept down. My father returned to the clearing; I climbed up on the wooden seat beside him, taking comfort from his size and strength. The lurking dangers faded back into the forest.

It was a trip to a storybook land.

"Now you know where your father spends his time," said my mother, as she pulled off my snow-filled overshoes and draped wet socks and mittens on the stovepipe to dry.

My father didn't hold much with folderol, but a few days before Christmas he drove the sledge up into the dooryard instead of the barnyard. Proudly perched on top of the load of logs was a tall, well-bushed-out hemlock — our Christmas tree. My father stood it up in a drift by the back door; the rest was up to my mother.

The tree was extra-special that year, because I knew what wilderness had been its home, how long and perilous its slow journey through the winter woods. I had been there.

My Aunt's Christmas

My Boston aunt was a most formidable person. She wore her serviceable skirts a little longer than most, her fingernails a little shorter.

Always choosing a straight-backed chair, Auntie sat in state, buttons properly done up, sensible shoes placed flat on the floor. Her impeccable shirtwaist was fastened with a cameo brooch, not a gray hair of her unbobbed head out of place.

It was her dark brown eyes that gave her away; they twinkled deep down with warmth and understanding.

"Don't pester your Aunt Harriet, now," my mother remonstrated as she bustled around, straightening doilies and knickknacks. "She's come a long way to make a Christmas visit, not to listen to childish prattle."

But I knew different; Aunt Harriet and I were kindred spirits from way back.

I sat beside her on the ottoman, smoothing my best plaid skirt, remembering not to cross my white-stockinged legs.

My mother had opened the parlor for this notable visit; a fire smoldered in the fireplace, keeping the chill just behind our shoulders.

"Tell me about Christmas when you were a little girl," I begged. We heard the rattle of teacups from the kitchen, smelled the hot-from-the-oven raisin buns.

My aunt turned the full attention of her elegant personage on me. Never had she held me on her lap, but she drew me close with a smile as she began her story.

"Christmas hadn't been a celebration very long when I was young," she said. "The first Christmas Eve I remember well was in 1870 when I was 10 years old. It had been a sunny and pleasant winter day, and I was to attend a party at the church. The festival's success back then depended on the weather. A foot of snow would keep most folks at home.

"But happily, it was a moon-shiny night, with the clear, crisp, dry cold that stimulates more than it chills," she continued. "In the vestry of the church, the long tables were set up with Sunday school settees instead of chairs. This meant that five people had to get up if someone wanted to sit down at the end, but nobody minded.

"All kinds of good things to eat were set out on the white cloth table covers — turkeys, cold roast beef, tongue, ham, bread (of

130

course it was homemade), big pats of freshly churned butter. There was coffee, tea, a great variety of cakes and little luxuries such as raisin clusters, sugarplums and candied ginger."

She paused, collecting her memories.

"The Christmas tree, crisscrossed with paper chains and strings of popcorn and cranberries, was decorated with hand-crafted ornaments and paper cornucopias filled with candy and nuts. Small gifts for us, the children, hung from the branches; homemade bags filled with marbles, embroidered handkerchiefs, miniature books, sachets, coin banks and tiny toys made of tin. Evergreens formed the major part of the decorations, since greens were always readily available then. Bunches of sumac and bittersweet, saved from the fall season, added color, along with ribbon garlands and flags.

"After the party," said my aunt, "sleighs and wagons were brought around to the church door, the horses snorting softly, their breath plumes of white in the still, cold air. Everybody was calling 'Merry Christmas' back and forth as we departed in the darkness for our homes. The smell of wood smoke tokened the warmth of the hearth ahead.

"That night, as the oil lamp flickered in the drafty chamber, I hung my stocking on the foot of my bed. The mantel seemed too far away. In the morning, it was filled with small gifts from Santa Claus," she said, casting me a wry glance. "There also was a handful of nuts, and down in the toe, a big orange.

"Our tree looked a lot like the one at the church, except we also had crocheted snowflakes, paper fans and a tussy-mussy or two made of paper flowers. Lot of folks wired tiny tapers to their tree, but my father pronounced it too dangerous.

"That was the year I received my first skates; my brother, your Uncle William, got a sled.

"Our Christmas dinner was much the same as it is now, but afterward, there was skating on the river above the dam where the ice was a foot thick. After an early light supper, we acted out charades, sang carols and played Shadows on the Wall."

Aunt Harriet finished her tea, shook hands with my mother and prepared to take her leave.

She didn't give me a kiss or even a hug, but we knew she had given me far more by sharing her memories, the sounds, the scents and the magic of a Christmas long ago.

The Sign of the Boot

My childhood Christmas days were all very much the same, but one stands out in memory. Or perhaps it is the highlights of several Christmases linked together, forming a pattern of security and happiness.

Waking in the big, square bedroom of the old farmhouse, there was little question in my mind whether Santa had come. He always did, and the long, brown stocking tied to the foot of the bed was bulging.

Snuggling down with it in the flannel sheets, I pulled out a small wind-up top, something soft wrapped in white tissue paper and tied with thin, red string, two walnuts in the shell, a few pieces of hard candy, and at the toe, a big orange.

Arranging my new treasures around me on the quilt, with my fingernail I scratched the skin of the orange to get the aroma. The smell of this special treat still reminds me of those icy Christmas mornings, the windows thick with white frost patterns, huge icicles girdled to the eaves like silver swords.

It was still very early. The house was quiet. Filled with excitement, I slipped stealthily down the front stairs in my long nightgown, opening the door into the deathly cold, unheated parlor to inspect the unused fireplace. This, I had been told, was the chimney Santa would use, and I had determined to check it out. Impressed on my remembrance still is the unmistakable big boot track I saw outlined on the faded carpet.

Back in bed, I found my hands still weren't strong enough to crack the two nuts by squeezing them together. Savoring the once-a-year treat of candy in bed, I was content to dally with my new possessions until my mother had the fire built up in the kitchen stove.

Carrying my clothes, I went again down the stairs, opening the door into the sitting room, getting my first look at what was under the tree, spotting the bright-red metal cart I had longed for.

Breakfast was as usual — some kind of hot cereal, toast and milk. The orange added the festive touch as the smell of roasting turkey wafted through the room.

The presents were opened before dinner, when my father had finished the morning chores, my mother could take a break from her cooking, and my married sister and her husband had arrived.

It was hard to wait. I wasn't allowed to play with my "big" present, the cart, even though I had seen it, until all the presents had been opened and admired.

My older sister gave out the gifts one at a time, reading the tags slowly and methodically at first, then speeding up to get to her own pile of packages.

I had two aunts, one who gave practical presents that came in the mail, another who brought, from Boston, unique and luxurious presents the Sunday before Christmas, placing them under the tree.

The big rectangular box my Boston aunt had left and which I had poked and prodded for almost a week, was an electric burning-pencil set, with squares of soft wood, stenciled pictures and even a set of paints.

I experimented with this novel and newfangled craft at the kitchen table, while my mother peeled small white onions, blue Hubbard squash and potatoes. Already on the stove, the plum pudding steamed away as my sister creamed butter and sugar for the hard sauce.

Wearing my new gift hat and mittens, I went with my brother-in-law to chop ice from the pond for freezing the ice cream. In the woodshed, he packed the ice with handfuls of rock salt in the old wooden freezer and slid in the covered metal container which held the ingredients for luscious peach ice cream.

As he cranked away, I used an old brick and a hammer to loosely crack the bag of mixed nuts for the wooden bowl, so they could be easily picked out as we lingered at the dinner table. It was cold in the woodshed, but both of us were looking forward to the moment when we could lick the ice cream from the dasher.

After dinner I joined the neighbors skating on the snow-cleared farm pond. The women did the dishes, smoothed out the crumpled wrapping paper to use next year, and arranged each person's presents in neat piles. The men made a trip to the barn, ostensibly to see to the animals, but actually, I knew, to enjoy what they called a Christmas "nip."

After a supper featuring turkey sandwiches, I was sent off to bed, with a scorching-hot brick, encased in a heavy woolen sock, to warm my feet. In the room below, I could hear the comforting murmur of voices and laughter as the adults played whist.

Outside, a light snow was falling, the gusty wind blowing whorls of flakes against the windows. I thought of all the rides I would take, all the chores I could do, with my new red cart. I planned what I would write on Jan. 1 on the first page of my new diary; and I again reveled in the wonder of the boot track on the parlor rug, a secret I would never tell.

Somehow I knew no one would believe in it as I did, and like fairies, if you can't believe in them, they don't exist.

The Song of the Sled

After Christmas came a week of outdoor play. We all had sleds of some sort, new or old. Mine was a small Speed-Away, but the next year I was due to inherit my sister's well-used but still swift Flexible Flyer.

Our farm had the best sliding slope, in fact it even had a name — Bellybump Hill. Not long after breakfast on those school vacation days, my friends would come scuffing up the lane, pulling their sleds, to go coasting. Marcella had an old dull-red, all-wooden sled with handholds in the runners, but no way to steer. Skinny's Flexible Flyer was the worse for wear. The steel bar on the front end was dented where he ran into a tree while going down standing up, a feat none of us ever really mastered. Our sleds were a treasured possession, our constant companions, unearthed from the back of the woodshed each November to spend the winter with us.

We were friends with the out-of-doors, spending the morning on the snow-covered hill, going home for lunch and returning. Mittens soggy, black buckle boots filled with snow, we made tracks, trails, sled trains and even a snow jump.

On those short winter days, the most rewarding part of spending a day in the cold, clear air was coming back to the warm kitchen, tired but invigorated and well-satisfied. We sat around the big black stove on the wooden chairs, mittens steaming on the stovepipe, drinking hot cocoa and eating soft molasses cookies.

My mother sat at the oilcloth-covered table, peeling potatoes or scraping carrots, listening to our feats of daring on the hillside.

As the years passed, we looked for new slopes to conquer. Down the road a piece was a long, winding hill with an S-curve, worn slick by autos and wagon sleds. Though there were only two houses on this 5-mile stretch of road, the first coaster to go down stood as a guard at the bottom to warn any oncoming cars of our presence. To vehicles coming up from behind, we would be easily visible, and would quickly outdistance their hazardous progress.

No ride in an amusement park ever quite equaled that high-speed descent on the ice-glazed hill as we hurtled through the chill depths of winter. We were in control, feeling the power of the speed in our hands. Frozen sled ropes coiled carefully beneath us, our faces were just inches from the iron-hard icy ruts as we flew along, bodies alive with vibrations from the runners. Eyes watering from the frigid airstream, we threw ourselves into the curve, steering hard.

Coasting to a stop, we marked our place on the snowdrift for the record and took our turn as guard before plodding the half-mile back up the hill.

Standing at the bottom, alone in the stillness, we watched for the next rider to come flying into view around the curve, eyes glued to the blur of the roadbed, boots a few inches off the ground. It was "sissy" to drag your feet, even if a rollover seemed imminent.

One January, we talked the leader of our young people's church group into a moonlight sliding party. The week before, we punched myriad holes in tin cans, fastened wires on for handles and stuck candles inside. These small, glowing lanterns were placed at the top and bottom of the hill and on the curve.

Ice glittered under the runners, tiny snow particles flew like diamond crystals in the luminous hush, stinging our eyelids, as the moon cast eerie shadows on the familiar landscape. The lanterns flashed by, tiny beacons in a sea of white, only the sound of snow-slicked steel breaking the stillness. The earth seemed to hold us close, the stars to draw near, as we made our perilous, swift descent.

Back in the church vestry, we drank hot cider and ate homemade doughnuts, with much stamping of feet to warm our tingling toes.

We were mere mortals again, awkward, shy, Arcadian, our clothes timeworn. But for a brief interval we had been gods on Mount Olympus, with the wings of Mercury, the strength of Ulysses, hearing faintly the pipes of Pan.

135

Watch Night

New Year's Eve was celebrated with Watch Night services, a gathering in the church vestry to say farewell to the old year, to greet the new.

A great deal of thought and planning went into this event; it held a place of stature in the life of the church and town. All celebrations were welcomed in the rather stark existence of a farm community back in Herbert Hoover's time. But this was an occasion encompassing far more than our tiny village — the Earth turned, the last page was torn from the familiar calendar, a new fresh year would dawn.

For years, the words "Watch Night" were spoken solemnly, almost with reverence.

To me, these last few hours of the year were shrouded in mystery until the December I was deemed old enough to attend. The hour was far too late, the activities too serious in content, too deep in concept for small children. Too, it was unthinkable that the profound reigning spirit of the gathering be shattered by a fretful or precocious young one. The sharp delineation that formerly existed between adults and children was never more evident than at this time.

Trepidation at being a part of my first Watch Night quickly faded into pleasure. The vestry looked as usual, the two big round furnaces crackling away, plenty of wood stacked alongside. Black-and-white crepe paper streamers were looped between the support columns. The familiar smell of freshly brewed coffee, Sunday school paste and drying bark mingled in the air.

We drew names for partners in a scavenger hunt, played paper and pencil games, sang songs.

About 11 o'clock, refreshments were served. Folks filled their punch or coffee cups, heaped green glass plates with sandwiches, cookies and cake, chattering softly in little groups all round the big, warm room.

The food made me sleepy. It had been an exciting night out, a lot of fun. Thinking it was all over, I was ready to go home, to savor in retrospect my first New Year's Eve celebration.

It was then the Watch Night service really began.

Chairs were placed in a large circle. Bulbs were unscrewed in the overhead fixtures so only one or two lights were left on. Silence fell as the minister took over. He consecrated the old year and the new, read Scriptures and an inspirational poem. Every five minutes he turned and looked at the big clock on the wall; all heads turned with him.

"It is now 25 minutes to midnight," he would intone; then, "It is now 20 minutes to the hour of midnight."

The tension and anticipation built to a frightening pitch. At midnight would the Earth be rent asunder? Would the stars fall from the sky?

We stood to sing with fervor from the hymnal, the words engraved forever in memory:

"The year is dying in the night,
Ring out, wild bells and let him die."

As the song died away, all joined hands. An old man tottered along the side of the room. His white robe was tattered, his mouth a grim line above a long white beard. He carried a real scythe, its long blade rusted, and an hourglass.

Like a spectre, he disappeared up the vestry stairs. He played his part well — we all knew who he was, but for those few seconds he was the old year passing away, Father Time personified.

The mood changed as down the stairs bounded yet another apparition, a rather pudgy man dressed as the baby New Year. This personage wore a voluminous white diaper fastened with a huge horse-blanket pin, a white shirt and a ludicrous ruffled bonnet. Across his chest was a banner emblazoned with cutout numbers: 1932.

He was here to stay, sitting among us amid laughter, nudges, looks of amazement and one or two reproachful glances and averted eyes (his feet and legs were bare).

When the hands of the clock stood at 11:55, we again joined hands and stood in silence as the last minutes ticked away toward the midnight's holy hour.

Suddenly, high above in the steeple the bell's deep tones pealed forth.

A bell's toll can sing of melancholy menace or golden delight; tonight it rang both — the death knell for the old year, a paean of jubilation for the new. Both sadness and joy mingled in every face.

A new year had dawned. In fellowship we sailed forth on the river of time. Childhood does not rue the years, but that night I learned that time is the one certain thing in the entire universe, moving inexorably past us.

Since that long-ago winter night, I have "seen in" many new years, some noisy and rowdy, others tastefully elegant, many quiet and serene.

But never have I been able to recapture the feeling of that first Watch Night service, when the church bells rang out in the frosty air, echoing across the snow, and the new year knocked gently on my heart.

Fanning the Flame

It had been a hard morning in the schoolroom. The long winter was taking its toll on weather-bound spirits, and "unsatisfactory deportment" would appear on many a report card.

Skinny had hidden a big icicle in his desk, which intermittently dripped on the floor, and Willie, miserable with chilblains, sniffled by the stove.

After lunch, eaten while sleet needled the windows, Miss Crosby passed out thin volumes of *The Rime of the Ancient Mariner* by Coleridge.

Priss raised her hand. "My mother says that book's too hard for us,"she said.

Miss Crosby gave her stock answer. "Becoming familiar with masterpieces of literature will help you develop true literary taste, a love of good reading and cultured original expression," she quoted.

Looking back, I can see a pattern in Miss Crosby's teaching, "a method to her madness," so to speak. When things looked their worst (which was always in February), she would delve deeper into the rich enchantments and richer humanity of the literary world, offering her own antidote, reading, to offset the rustic boisterousness in the confinement of the stuffy schoolroom.

Unfortunately, we weren't ready for this flight into higher literary circles. While an older class would have listened entranced (she had a flair for drama), most of us, at this point in the day, would have benefited far more from a spirited game of musical chairs.

Beside me sat Maurice, a shock of bear-greased hair falling over one eye. Behind his book, he had his peashooter ready, loaded with tiny balls of putty. He cast me a conspiratorial lopsided grin as he waited for the teacher to become involved in the lesson.

Without incident, we came to the last two lines of Part I — "Why lookst thou so? With my crossbow I shot the albatross."

This was too much for Maurice. He let fly his putty ball, which hit the stovepipe with a loud "ping." We all laughed, and for just a second, I thought Miss Crosby would break down, too, but instead she collared Maurice and assigned him to sit in the woodbox for punishment.

To rein in the rest of us, she began to read Part II.

It was a losing battle. As she read:

"Water, water everywhere
And all the boards did shrink;
Water, water everywhere,
But not a drop to drink . . ."

All eyes turned to Skinny's desk, where the icicle water was now trickling out in a small stream, soaking the oiled floorboards.

Averting her eyes, Miss Crosby quickly finished up the last few stanzas of Part II, threw the diminished remains of the icicle out the door, and assigned Skinny to the other half of the woodbox.

She gave us closely hoarded drawing materials and retired to her desk, where she kept a love confessions magazine in the middle drawer.

Old Crosseye knew when to throw in the towel, but she was far from defeated. Week after week, she continued to guide us through some of the best works of the great poets and writers.

Though much of it eluded us, the graphic pictures painted on our young minds as we groped for knowledge, the beauty of the language, and the vague conception of a deeper meaning in life, broadened our horizons far beyond the boot-scarred door of that long-ago country schoolhouse.

Valentine Verse

After I became a good reader, rhymes formed patterns in my head, falling unprompted into place like the prisms of a kaleidoscope.

February 14 was approaching; this year as always, my Valentines would have to be made by hand. Having seen a few store-bought Valentine cards, I knew they were often in rhyme, and leaned heavily on couplets like "you-blue," "mine-Valentine," and "dear-near."

These seemed simple enough. I decided to give full rein to my hovering Muse and liven up my homemade epistles with a few verses of my own.

It was a big year for sentiment. Instead of the usual white grocer's paper, the Valentine postbox in the schoolroom was covered in hand-ruffled pink crepe paper. Old Crosseyes had given us each a whole sheet of stiff, red paper to make cutout hearts, and these were displayed all over the room, from the windowpanes to the water pail. In addition, two of the eighth-graders were secretly engaged. He had given her the ring he won playing Pitch Till You Win at the county fair; she had let him keep her best embroidered handkerchief.

I spent several evenings at the kitchen table with paper, scissors, flour paste, doilies and a cigar box of decorations saved over the years. Writing the verses was even easier than I thought.

"To Priss, a sweet little miss"; "For Grace with the pretty face"; "Harry, Harry, who will you marry?"; and "Good looking Will, you are never a pill" — these rolled off my mind slick as water off a duck's back.

"It is such bliss, to know Maurice," seemed slightly extravagant, but after all, it was the time of year to put your heart into it.

Skinny could in no way be called a ninny, so I had to use his real name, coming up with: "The girls all hustle, to sit next to Russell." This wasn't entirely true, either, since Skinny usually had a frog, a dried hen's foot or a piece of strung garlic in his pocket.

I was satisfied with "Fair little Miriam, puts the boys in delirium" and "Malcolm, Malcolm, sweeter than talcum."

A verse for Miss Crosby came last. Nothing seemed to rhyme

Your charming Grace,
Sweet Valentine,
Has captured
this fond Heart
of Mine.

with "Crosby." Time was running out, so I settled for her title, which immediately rhymed with "creature." What kind of creature? I had already used the word "handsome." "Beautiful" and "lovable" seemed superfluous; she was not the Lily Maid of Astalot.

I decided to use the highest praise my father could give, his criteria when buying a new horse. Inside the folded paper card I pasted an extra turtledove and wrote:

"Happy Valentine's Day to my teacher,
A well-timbered, high-stepping creature."

The next morning I deposited my somewhat sticky offerings in the Valentine postbox, where most of the pupils were congregated before Miss Crosby rang the bell. The boys might only deposit one or two cards for their favorite girls (and these possibly signed "guess who"), so they slid them in on the sly. Like the rest of the girls, I had one for everybody.

After lunch, a "postman" was chosen by drawing slips of paper from a chalk box. Miriam was the lucky one. Anticipation rippled like waves through the warm, stuffy room as mail was placed on our desks. Though one or two fellow students seemed a little doubtful about the true meaning of my rhymes, most were intrigued and impressed.

Miss Crosby, as always, received the most Valentines, and she was all atwitter over so many accolades. Suddenly, she sat very still and gave me a baleful look. When she arranged her Valentines artistically along the window sills, mine was not among them.

Something must have been wrong with my verse. I looked up "well-timbered" in the dictionary and found it meant "sturdily built." That was valid, all right, nothing wrong there.

After school, I sat down in the kitchen rocker. The room smelled of newly ironed handkerchiefs and simmering turnips.

Would you like to be called a "high-stepper?" I asked my mother, who was, I figured in the same social class as Miss Crosby.

Accustomed to my rhetorical flights of fancy, my mother only chuckled as she deftly crimped the crust on a molasses-apple pie.

"Land, no," she said, "not unless I was a dance-hall girl."

So that was it! A high-stepping horse was one thing, a woman another! Atonement would have to be made.

That night I fashioned another Valentine.

"True greetings, late but glad,
For the nicest teacher I ever had," it said.

At first glance, this might sound too lavish, but I wasn't gilding the lily. You could carry poetic license just so far.

She was the *only* teacher I ever had.

143

Lost at Sea

The schoolroom, in all ways except sleeping, was our home away from home. In that one room, we learned our lessons, practiced music, worked on sewing or manual training, struggled through our punishments, ate our lunch. Until we went to high school in a large neighboring town, we had never heard of an "assembly," a gym or a lunchroom.

While several grades worked on an arithmetic assignment, the teacher would hear the reading, geography or history of another grade. It was hard to concentrate on our take-aways while the teacher outlined the battle of Bull Run on the blackboard.

"Eyes on your own work!" she would snap, rapping her pointer on the chalk tray.

Miss Crosby was strict. She had to be. Our school was a little world of its own, set off in a field with woods behind, and she was the only adult in it.

It was rare indeed for parents to come to the school, and it usually meant bad news, like the time Porky's father fell out of the apple tree and ruptured his spleen. Porky was whisked away in his uncle's carryall and not seen again until after the funeral.

The only respites Miss Crosby had were when the music teacher came twice a month or during the monthly visits of the nurse. While we rollicked through *A Capital Ship for an Ocean Trip*, yawned over *Flow Gently, Sweet Afton*, or while the nurse inspected our fingernails and looked in our ears, she would get a chance to leave the room.

The superintendent of schools, a thin man with pince-nez glasses, came once a year, but on that day, old Crosseye (as we called her in secret) was busier than ever, all flushed up to show what a good teacher she was.

One winter afternoon, as snowflakes drifted down outside the windows, the two upper grades began reading *The Wreck of the Hesperus* by Longfellow.

The room was somnolent, stuffy with the smell of wet wool, drying rubber boots and singed bread from the stove where we had toasted our sandwiches at lunch.

How many apples John would have left if he gave six to Mary and three to Bob paled to unimportance as I was transported to the reef of Norman's Woe, reveling in the drama as,

"He wrapped her warm in his seaman's coat,
Against the stinging blast;
He cut a rope from a broken spar
And bound her to the mast . . ."

My reverie was broken when Priscilla (Miss Priss, as we sometimes called her), raised her hand.

"Elinor's listening again," she smirked.

"Well, miss," boomed Crosseyes, "if you like this poem so well, you may memorize it and recite it for the class tomorrow."

That night after my mother called "lights out," I lit a forbidden candle, and huddling under the quilts, began to memorize the many stanzas of the poem. The wind had risen, and snow was hissing against the windowpanes as I was once again transported to the Northeast gale off the Massachusetts coast.

The next day in school, the rhythmic tale was easy to remember. Miss Crosby had to prompt me a few times, but she was mollified. At recess, she even looked the other way when I stuffed a big snowball down Miss Priss' neck.

Up from the Earth

The farm sprang into life in April. The day the first furrow fell back from the plowshare was a special occasion. Dark brown and moist, the earth rippled over the moldboard, leaving a deep scar across the length of the field.

The horses, Fannie and Charlie resplendent in harness mended and polished in the early darkness of winter afternoons, strained into the traces. They were well-rested, as eager as I to be out in the spring sunshine. They tossed their heads at the robins, sparrows and grackles hopping in the newly turned dirt, as the swathes of plowed ground grew ever wider.

Worm can in hand, I followed behind, competing with the birds. The fishing season had opened, and there were trout in the brook that would rise to a lively worm.

From far out at the furrow's end, I could look back at the homeplace, spread out before me. The wind poured down, setting adance the barely budded boughs of elms, tossing into a frenzy the willows by the pond. The new lambs leaped sidewise like coiled springs in the barn pasture, and the dishtowels on the clothesline blew straight out like white flags, surrendering to the gale.

On the town road, I heard a car horn, and saw the driver beckoning me over. My mother was always cautioning me about raggedy tramps and villainous gypsies, but the man was well-turned out and genial as a judge.

"What's that you're picking up, sis," he said, "worms?"

I showed him the tangled ball wriggling in the coffee can.

"I bet I have a hundred," I boasted.

"I'll give you 50 cents for them," he said. Flabbergasted at this munificence, I handed them over, and was launched into business.

My mother was impressed with the two quarters, and agreed I could paint a "Worms for Sale" sign and nail it up at the end of the driveway on Saturday.

All the rest of that afternoon and the next, I followed the plow, pulling worms from the clods of soil. That night I put covers on the three well-filled cans, storing them on a bench in the woodshed. With a nail and hammer, I punched a few holes in each can so the worms could breathe.

I fell asleep anticipating the money I would make the next day. But in the morning, every worm was gone. They had escaped through the air holes, my mother said, stifling a smile. I was chopfallen, and moped around the rest of the day. At noon, the hired man grinned at me. "Been catching many worms lately?" He slapped his knee and guffawed, plunging me deeper into despondency. Along with the worms, I had lost caste.

My father was always tired and uncommunicative on plowing nights, from sitting on the hard, jolting iron seat all day, but that night as he led the horses to the barn he called me over, fishing an object from his vest pocket. Silently, he handed me a perfectly shaped Indian arrowhead. I knew what it was. In one of the drawers of the big oak desk was a tin tobacco box, half-filled with similar artifacts.

"But don't you want it to put in the tobacco can?" I asked.

"It's time you had a collection of your own," he said.

I began haunting the fields again, but now, Indian drums beat in my head, luring me on as my eyes searched for arrowheads.

I never found one, but as I became involved in a new treasure hunt, the ill-starred misadventure with the worms faded into the mists of childhood memory, just as my father had known it would.

Spring Greens

We recognized spring by the plants more than by the unpredictable weather, or even the wedge of geese in the sky.

The earth warmed, the growing things sprang forth, responding to a force that never failed. The elusive mayflower, hidden violets, the delicate white star of anemone were all colorful markers of a long-awaited spring. Best of all were the cowslips.

The cowslip, which some people call marsh marigold, grows in swampy places, its bright-yellow blossoms bursting like a joyous cry along the bare, brown woods. It was a spring diet staple, our first taste of a fresh vegetable for many months.

The year came when I was sent off alone to gather the first cowslips. They were the most flavorful and tender before the blossoms appeared, and my mother knew just the right time.

She was bogged down in the middle of spring-cleaning the china closet.

"Take a clean grain bag," she said, "and be sure to wear your overshoes." She had a mortal dread of wet feet.

I wasn't loath to go. Always ready to follow the call of waters flowing, I would also get to carry a sharp knife. Pulling the plants up by the roots would soon put an end to the harvest.

My unbuckled overshoes flapping, I slogged along, across the bare pasture, past the grove, drawn by the breath of early ferns.

All along the edge of the bog I cut the tender leaves and stems, storing them in the bag. I had almost enough for a "good mess of greens" when I saw a particularly fine clump deep in the quagmire.

As I stepped into the mud, my feet sank quickly. I sliced off my prize, and felt the mud around my knees. The earth was drawing me close. I pictured my head slowly disappearing under the muck. Would I sink all the way to China?

In desperation, I fell forward and grasped onto a huge tussock, pulling my feet out one by one with a sickening, sucking sound. The overshoes were gone.

"Heaven help us," scolded my mother when she saw me, well-covered with slimy black mud that had started to dry. "I've a good mind to put you right in the set tubs." These deep, square soapstone sinks were where I had been given a bath as a little girl.

She drew in her horns, though, when she saw the half-bushel of cowslips, and let me wash up at the sink. She put my gingham dress to soak, along with the rest of my clothes.

When my brother-in-law, Walter, came home from work, she sent us off to retrieve the overshoes. As the bright day drowsed on the hills, the sunset scattered gold on the twilight stream. From a swaying cattail, a red-winged blackbird sang his "tur-a-lee," a prelude for the peepers, which would soon begin their evening concert.

Walter dug around with a rake and pulled out the overshoes one by one. The mud pool settled back, dark, still, with little bubbles rising. For a shivery moment I lingered, half-expecting the jeweled sword Excalibur to rise from the depths, or worse yet, a pale white hand.

That night for supper we ate fried ham with milk gravy, hot biscuits and mounds of the slightly bitter, woodsy-tasting cowslip greens, cooked with a piece of salt pork. In spite of the mishap, I received an approving look from my father for putting food on the table.

As such things go on a farm, the site received a name. Ever after it was called "the quick-mud pool" and given a wide berth.

"It's funny the sheep never fell in it," I said.

"Sheep's got more brains," said my father. My mother patted my arm, and at dessert time, served me an extra big piece of rhubarb pie.

The Forest Fire

In the days of early spring, we worked hard in school, as a last gasp for a good report card and promotion to the next grade. After the middle of May, nothing we did mattered very much, because Miss Crosby had already made up her mind and marked it down.

As we all buckled down that April day, the schoolroom was quiet, except for an occasional shuffling of feet, a cough or a sniffle. The stove had been lit to take the chill off, but had burned down to a few glowing coals. Outside, a bird sang from the top of the old maple tree by the wall, and on its white wooden pole the flag fluttered lazily.

Suddenly, shattering the quiet morning, the church bell began to ring. As one man, we threw down our pencils and dashed to the tall windows, peering at the high white steeple visible through the budding trees as though a message would appear

We all knew what it meant — there was a fire somewhere in town.

The word "fire" struck terror and excitement in all our hearts. The blackened skeleton of Widow Perkins house still stood on the valley road, a mute and sobering reminder of what a fire could do.

The bell tolled frantically on. How could a cadence that on Sunday morning echoed so welcoming and sweet now sound so ominous?

Miss Crosby joined us at the window. "Now, don't worry, it's probably just a little brush fire," she soothed. As usual, she dismissed the older boys so they could go help put it out, along with every able-bodied man in town.

They raced down the road just as we heard the bell of the old pumper truck as it left the town garage. Close behind them ran Willie, a messenger sent to return with news of the fire's location.

The pumper didn't pass the school, so at least four children could breathe a sigh of relief — it wasn't their property in danger.

Willie returned, panting. "It's in the woods behind Cole's house," he gasped. My stomach turned over, and all eyes turned my way. That was my house.

At noon recess, we could smell the sweet, heart-sickening wood smoke, an odor we had learned to fear while still in long dresses.

The afternoon dragged on. Old Crosseyes knew I was worried and went easy on me. "Don't worry," she said. "If it was serious, they'd come and get you." I knew this was not true. Children had no place in the adult world when disaster struck.

As I hurried home after school, I could see the huge gray clouds of smoke rolling up. My mother was not in the kitchen, an ominous sign. I found her at the edge of the pasture, her hands clutching a fence post as if for support, watching the fire crown from tree to tree at the end of the field, as men with shovels worked feverishly on a firebreak.

Late in the afternoon, some ladies from the church brought the coffee urn, and they helped my mother make sandwiches in our kitchen. I rode in the back of the pickup to deliver the food to the men, so close I could feel the searing heat and hear the crackle and roar as the fire raced through the winter-dried woods.

Until I fell asleep, I heard the thump of the engine, which was steadily pumping water from the brook. It was a comforting sound, like a noisy dragon keeping the enemy at bay.

In the morning, the fire was out. The wind had changed, my father said, "A lucky thing," and I could see how concerned he had been.

I could tell, too, how proud he was to have fought and won. It showed in his red-rimmed eyes and in the set of his shoulders under the torn and sooty flannel shirt. He, too, was a force of nature.

"There's good in everything," said my mother. "The burn-over will make next year's blueberry crop the best ever."

As I did my chores, the smell of the fire hung over everything. Wise in the way of animals, the horses rolled their eyes and were skittish. I hugged my pet lamb, thankful he was still safe in the big old barn.

The horror of yesterday made today's sun brighter, the grass greener, life a royal thing.

About the Author

Elinor Frances Cole was born on February 23, 1923, in Haverhill, Massachusetts , the third daughter and last child of Harry Lee and Ethel (Killam) Cole. She lived on the family farm in West Boxford until the age of 26 –"raised," as she writes in her introduction to this book, "in an atmosphere of proverbs, superstitions, homemade bread and the New Deal."

Elinor worked as a secretary and assistant editor for the *Andover Townsman*; at the same time, she was a stringer-correspondent for the *Lawrence Daily Eagle* and assisted the American Red Cross, driving an ambulance between Lawrence and Boston. She also did volunteer work at the Bedford Hospital.

The year 1949 proved an important one. Elinor moved to Marblehead where she met and married Elwin Carleton Bemis, a real estate agent; they settled down in West Boxford. Her husband died in an automobile accident four years later, leaving her alone with Christopher, 4, Jon, 2, and Michael, 1. When Michael turned 5, Mrs. Bemis taught a private kindergarten for four years, and took courses in education, having always wanted to be a teacher.

Mrs. Bemis taught in the Boxford public schools for eight years. When her mother died in 1969, she returned to her childhood home in West Boxford, accompanied by her children, in order to be with her father. In 1976, her son Michael moved to Maine. "I came to see if I liked it, and I did."

In Kennebunk, Mrs. Bemis continued to pursue her newspaper writing, at the *York County Coast Star*, where she worked as a collator, correspondent, proofreader, and editorial assistant. Now retired, in a manner of speaking, she continues as a correspondent and columnist for the paper.

She types on a 10-year-old Swintec in her office. Each column takes about three days to complete: research, if necessary, and writing the first day; smoothing out the second day; and reading and writing it all out on the third.

Mrs. Bemis lives a very secluded life – by choice. "I like solitude," she says. Wading at the seashore several times a week proves inspiring to her creative enterprise. Indeed, the beach, in Mrs. Bemis' eye, is a good place to write: it has, in her words, "an aesthetic atmosphere."

Her columns have attracted a large following, and she regularly receives letters praising her ability to recreate childhood scenes. The diaries she kept from age 10 to 16 provide some of the material for her writings. "I don't live in the past," Mrs. Bemis states, "but I love to write about the past."